Understanding
Complex Organizations

ELEMENTS OF SOCIOLOGY
A Series of Introductions

Understanding Complex Organizations

Thomas E. Drabek

University of Denver

J. Eugene Haas

University of Colorado

WM. C. BROWN COMPANY PUBLISHERS
Dubuque, Iowa

SOCIOLOGY SERIES

Consulting Editors

Ann Lennarson Greer
University of Wisconsin-Milwaukee

Scott Greer
Northwestern University

46013

HM
3 P3l4
D7
D 95u

Printed in the United States of America

Contents

Foreword

FROM its outset the United States has been a society of organizations. Observing the unique importance of organizations in American life, the Frenchman Alexis de Tocqueville wrote the following description in 1833:

Americans of all ages, all stations in life, and all types of disposition are forever forming associations. There are not only commercial and industrial associations in which all take part, but others of a thousand different types—religious, moral, serious, futile, very general and very limited, immensely large and very minute.*

Through the years the organization scene has become even more variegated. Organizations are intricately bound up with the life of the nation; no individual can escape their influence. There are organizations to preserve values and those to change them. Organizations advocate causes from natural childbirth to the right to die with dignity. And, there has been a recent upsurge of voluntary action organizations challenging established business, educational, and governmental institutions. More than ever before, organizations are where the action is.

It seems reasonable, therefore, that American students should be introduced to the study of society through a study of its organizations. Like no other book I know, *Understanding Complex Organizations* does precisely that. Using organizations as a key to the understanding of social organization generally, the authors introduce students to sociology through an understanding of the kinds of organizations which are important in everyday life. Students not only learn what organizations are like and why, they also learn how individuals can cope with organizations and with an organized society.

Written at a level the beginner in sociology can understand, this book combines relevance with an insightful analysis of the central concepts and recent trends in the discipline of sociology. Furthermore, (unlike so many other organizations texts) it is not focused narrowly on industrial and business organizations, but amply treats voluntary organizations, including their role in forming public policy and effecting social change.

Understanding Complex Organizations can serve equally well as a first book in sociology (combined with other materials) or a first book in organizations (along with an empirical project or case studies of particular organizations). In either case, this text will excite students to think sociologically about the events and relationships which impinge on their lives at every turn.

James R. Wood
Indiana University

*Alexis de Tocqueville, *Democracy in America.* Translated by George Lawrence and edited by J. P. Mayer. (Garden City, N.Y.: Doubleday and Co., Inc., 1969), p. 513.

Preface

Why read a book entitled *Understanding Complex Organizations?* Even more important—why write such a book when numerous analyses of organizational research are available already? We took these questions seriously at the outset. Now that the task is completed we want to highlight five central themes that guided us throughout.

First, unlike most others, this book was written for newcomers to the social sciences—those unfamiliar with its logics, methods, and rhetorics. But in contrast to emphasizing technical jargon and endless definitions, we have presented in as informal a manner as possible, a way of thinking about life within large organizations. Thus, we have sought to communicate an imagery—a style of thought and analysis of the complex behavior patterns in which we participate everyday, but rarely think about much.

Second, we have provided an historical context for the organizational society in which most of us will live out our days. America was not always comprised of the dense organizational networks we take for granted today. Why did they emerge? Here again is an image—one of persons seeking to construct weapons of a sort, so as to enhance their personal wealth at times, and at others to curb the powers of a "common enemy."

Third, how are organizations to be analyzed? While greater rigor of analysis is possible only through more indepth study of organizations, we have sought to guide newcomers into an analytical technique. Basic principles and concepts that are widely shared by sociologists are described and illustrated. Conflict and strain, as well as cooperation and consensus, are emphasized, however. In contrast to those who view organizational participants as rule-following robots, we have pictured more active creatures who frequently find considerable room for movement within the limits enforced by officials. But this is more true in some organizations than in others. So we have explicated several major dimensions in which organizations vary. Some *are* more authoritarian than others, for example.

Fourth, throughout our presentation another theme is constant—organizations do not exist in vacuums. They both act upon and are constrained by environmental forces of varied types. Interorganizational relationships as well as other environmental sectors are explored. Layer upon layer of vertical authority structures constrain organizational officials today. Yet, paralleling their subordinates, whose actions appear so irrational at times, persons at the top are engaged in continual renegotiation efforts calculated to expand or at least maintain existing levels of autonomy, security, and prestige.

Finally, we raise throughout the book, but especially in the last chapter, the most fundamental question—what meaning might this analysis have for you? It is our belief that this work—like study of the social sciences in general, or for that matter the various disciplines within the natural sciences and the humanities—can provide a unique imagery and logical framework for addressing the most fundamental questions that confront any human being. Who are you? Why are you the way you are? Only by pondering such questions with the enhanced rigor offered by the multiple frameworks proposed by various academic disciplines can you attain a greater capacity for freedom. And so we seek to motivate you to pursue seriously what is undoubtedly the most important question of all—what do you want to do with your life? To the extent that this little book provides such stimulation, we will consider it a success.

As with any such enterprise, numerous individuals assisted us in a great many ways

during the completion of this project. Deanna Nervig translated our working drafts into final copy with precision and speed for which we are most grateful. Drabek was assisted by the highly competent secretarial staff of the Department of Sociology at the University of Denver. Human Ecology Research Services, Inc., provided partial financial support for the reproduction of our working drafts. We also wish to acknowledge our appreciation for the help provided by Scott and Ann Greer, the series editors. Special thanks to Jim Wood for his comments and willingness to contribute. We appreciated Dick Burkey's thoroughness in commenting on our early draft. Bob Nash and many others at Wm. C. Brown Company were of continual assistance throughout the production phase.

Finally, to our families—especially our wives, Ruth Ann and Mary Helen—we offer special thanks for numerous insightful criticisms of this manuscript and the emotional support provided as we struggled to complete it.

T.E.D.
J.E.H.

1 | Organizations Are Everywhere

IMAGINE for a moment that we are at the corner of Market and Powell streets in San Francisco, California. It's noon. The sidewalks are crowded and persons bustle past us in every direction in a seemingly unorganized manner. Where are they going in such a rush? How will they know when they get there?

What we are seeing is not unique to San Francisco. We might just as well be at the corner of Ninth and Plum streets in Cincinnati, Bourbon and St. Ann in New Orleans, Alamo and Houston in San Antonio, or Sixteenth and Court in Denver. Denver? O.K. Let's shift our observation point to there.

It's still noon. Mobs of people rush past us as we watch while sitting atop a low cement wall which encloses a small outdoor ice skating rink. Looking in any direction, up or down Sixteenth Street or sideways along Court Street, we see people moving. Wait! Some are stopping. Now they are joined by others who stop at the corner too. Cars speed past. Crowds on each corner grow larger. Suddenly, the cars stop and the people move into the street. Some go straight across, but others go diagonally—right through the middle. Of course, they're simply doing the *Barnes' Dance* which originated here many years ago through the creative genius of the man with the red and green eyes, as Henry Barnes—who once served as the Mile High city's chief traffic engineer—labeled himself.[1]

Now the cars are moving again as a few people quickly scramble to safety. Crowds again form on each corner, and the pattern is repeated. Over and over again throughout the day, the movements of hundreds of automobiles and pedestrians are coordinated along this street. Remarkably, collisions between them are rare. Their behavior, when viewed in this context, is highly patterned. Cars move sixty seconds, then stop while people move. Activities that appear disorganized at first, suddenly reveal a high degree of structure.

What provides the structure? Why do crowds gather at each corner and then suddenly begin to move? Structure emerges in the behavior of this collection of individuals, most of whom are strangers to one another, each going his separate way, through a simple sign. Each has his private thoughts, purposes and destination. But through a simple sign, a traffic light, the

1. Henry A. Barnes, *The Man With the Red and Green Eyes* (New York: Dutton, 1965).

1

privately motivated movements of hundreds become highly patterned.

How do they know when they get to where they are going? Through other signs. What kinds? Let's look down this street and see. "World Savings"—know what that is? "Paramount"—know what's in there? What about this one—"Grab a Bite"? "Fashion Bar"?—in case there is any doubt, dresses in the window quickly communicate to us that this is not a place to order a beer. And glancing down Court Street we see "Continental Airlines." Looking to the left— "Continental Trailways"; and so it goes. From this one spot we can see many more signs which designate places to buy wigs, sporting goods, cameras, eyeglasses, and, if you are interested, even a quick printing job. Moving down Sixteenth Street we notice two tall buildings looming above all others. Atop one is a sign—"Security Life"; and a single "W" designating "Western Federal Savings," is affixed on the other. In many societies we might expect these locations, high above the crowds, to be allocated to religious symbols. Not so here, at least as these participants *verbally* define religion.

Up and down the street are signs. While some are large and others small, each identifies a separate behavior setting. That is, a spatial location where a particular type of activity takes place. Only in locations designated as restaurants or cafeterias will we find lunch being served. And while we are surrounded by fishing poles, tents, boots, and back packs, in a building marked "sporting goods," lunch would be a long wait, unless of course you prefer the freeze dried variety.

At each of these locations, if we were to stop and watch for awhile, we could describe the behavior patterns among persons just as we did at the street corner. However, in contrasting that rather simple "stop and go" behavior pattern among pedestrians and automobiles, a restaurant activity pattern, or that of a sporting goods store, is much more complex. In such settings we would find several interrelated behavior patterns which persist simultaneously. These more complex interaction systems we call *organizations*.

Organizations are everywhere. And think of the variety. Bus depots, hotels, newspapers, fire departments, churches, and places to go to buy things—pizza, beer, motorcycles, haircuts, and wigs. If you really want to get the point, let your fingers do the walking. Seriously! Most of us don't appreciate the wide variety of organizations that exist today. Spend some time looking through the Yellow Pages and you will be surprised. Every page, like the listing reprinted in Figure 1.1, identifies organization after organization and specifies where you can find it.

Through signs, persons locate the activity setting they are seeking. These signs, like the traffic signal, provide structure to their behavior. Let's explore that idea just a minute. In our exploration, let's continue to observe behavior as if we were outsiders. Only in this way can we highlight the patterns which are too easily hidden from us, because usually we are participants and take all of this for granted. By making problematic what we customarily take for granted, we can gain much insight into social organizations of all types.

RUNABOUT PERIODS

Imagine that we are now in a helicopter looking down on our observation corner at Sixteenth and Court Streets in Denver,

Figure 1.1. Organizational Roll Books—The Yellow Pages*

Looking under the F's in the Laramie-Rock River, Wyoming, directory we find the following categories:

Fabric Shops	Formal Wear—Rental
Fairgrounds	Foundries
Farm Equipment	Fraternal Organizations
Farm Equipment—Repairing & Supplies	Fraternities & Sororities
Financing	Freight Forwarding
Fire Alarm Systems	Frozen Food Locker Plants
Fire Departments	Frozen Foods—Processors
Fire Extinguishers	Frozen Foods—Retail
Fire Protection Equipment	Fruits & Vegetables—Wholesale
Fireplace Equipment—Dealers	Funeral Directors
First Aid Supplies	Fur Business—Retail
Fish Hatcheries	Fur Skin Dealers & Brokers
Fishing Bait	Furnaces—Heating
Fishing Tackle—Dealers	Furniture
Fix-It Shops	Furniture Renting & Leasing
Floor Materials—Dealers	Furniture Repairing & Refinishing
Floor Waxing, Polishing & Cleaning	Furniture—Unfinished
Florists—Retail	Furniture—Used
Foods—Ready to Serve	

*Titles reprinted from the *Laramie-Rock River Telephone Directory*, Cheyenne, Wyoming: The Mountain States Telephone and Telegraph Company, November, 1972.

Colorado. It is 5:00 A.M., and few persons are visible. As we approach 6:30 A.M., the number increases. But by 7:30 A.M., long lines of cars are creeping along. The volume slows a bit, but picks up again about 4:30 P.M. Just like our crowd moved into the street when the light changed, people seem to exit from every door around and jump into their cars. Our second "runabout period" has begun, to use a term coined by R. Drabek. The streets will be less crowded shortly, until—yes, the same time tomorrow. Unless, of course, tomorrow happens to be Sunday.

And so, day after day, from our helicopter, we could note this pattern. If we sharpened our focus a bit and began to identify persons as individuals, we would discover that this is not a pattern of random movement. This is not a crowd simply moving into the downtown area. Rather, each individual is headed for a particular organization, i.e., a special activity setting.

Look down. What do you see? Here are several people entering a building—"B-A-N-K," the sign says. Here are others entering another one—"Denver Public Library."

Each of these are special locations wherein only certain types of activities occur. Checks are cashed at banks, not libraries. And don't try to return a book at a location designated "bank." If we watched them day after day, many of the same persons would return to the identical locations and participate in activities similar to those they had *performed* on previous days.

Performed? That may sound strange in this context. Yet, think about it. From our helicopter vantage point above the city, it is as if we are looking down on hundreds of theater stages.[2] Each has a different script and program of activity. Each day "the actors" return to play their "parts." They "play" throughout the day; but then, as suddenly as they arrived, most begin to exit, almost as if on a cue from the sun. And another "runabout period" begins.

Each of these "stages," is a rather specialized activity pattern. The various actors engage in similar activities each day depending upon which stage they are located. Thus, their interaction has similar content each day. The same activity patterns reappear day after day, after day, even though some of the individual actors may die, move away, or decide to join another "stage." On stages labeled "restaurant," actors continue to prepare foods while on "sporting goods" stages others unpack ski poles and gloves. Thus, within this or any other community, we find structure and pattern in the sense that actors play parts within complexes of organizations, each of which has its own particular activity pattern. In your "mind's eye," try and picture this imagery for a second. "Look down" on your city and "see" the various "theaters" which are in motion simultaneously. Now let's drop down a bit and focus in on one of these.

ON STAGE

We are still in our helicopter, but considerably lower. At this level we can concentrate our attention on a single stage. We note its sign—"Central Bank and Trust Company." The "runabout period" has just ended. Our influx of actors who moved into the downtown area a short while ago are now situated. Each is on his separate stage playing his particular part. And we—to push this imagery further—are the audience, awed and stimulated by the speed with which this massive number became located into these varied activity patterns.

Here comes another car down the street. It is turning off the street and now is moving right along the side of the bank beneath us. It has stopped behind two other cars which are behind a third one. Who are they? Why are they staying in their cars? Let's leave our place in the audience for a moment and go down "on stage" and ask.

"Madam—excuse me. Ah, we are doing a study of this bank. And, ah, could you answer a couple of questions for us?"

"Sure! If I can."

"Well, ah, we were wondering why you are here? I mean, we've not seen you here before."

"Well, I need some money."

"Oh, do you have a friend here?"

"No, I just want to cash a check."

"Oh, O.K. Thanks for your time."

As we depart our interviewee might be thinking to herself: "Wierd! I wonder what that was all about? Gad, what's taking that guy so long. Come on. Come on. I don't want to sit here all day."

The cars ahead move out. She pulls forward, and puts a small piece of paper into a box that the person inside the bank pushed out after she stopped. The box is pulled back; now out it comes again. She reaches inside, picks up several green papers which we recognize as money, and drives away. Neither person spoke a word!

Perhaps this seems wierd to you too. What is so special about a person cashing a check? Well, in a sense, nothing. Nothing

2. This mode of analysis using the imagery of the stage has been developed exceptionally well by Erving Goffman in several books. See, for example, *The Presentation of Self in Everyday Life* (Garden City, N.Y.: Doubleday-Anchor, 1959).

that is, until we think about it for a minute. Why would one stranger give money to another stranger? How could such a transaction take place without either speaking a word?

Of course the answer is obvious to us who know the script for this stage. The obvious becomes problematic only when we find ourselves in a foreign culture and don't know the rules. Which line do we get into inside a bank in Florence, Italy, or Bern, Switzerland? But there is more to it than just language. Remember? Neither person spoke a word. Perhaps they had never seen each other before this either. Yet each knew exactly what to do. How? Because each understood the normative expectations that defined the appropriate range of behaviors for individuals acting these two parts. The norms, or expected ways of behaving, apply whether you personally know the individual acting the other part or not. These norms, then, similar to our traffic signal, guide the behavior of our actors. They permit hundreds to quickly go through the drive-up window of the bank throughout the day. None need to know the teller personally. Instead, each knows the script.

If we followed our female interviewee away from the bank for awhile, we might see her repeat a similar pattern of activity several times. There she goes into a building whose front windows are filled with dresses, coats, and shoes. Speaking to no one, she picks up a coat; gives the clerk a small card; signs her name on the charge slip; and walks out. And so it goes, as she moves past building after building, entering only a few.

Think of how the participants in the building communicate to persons walking past. How do they know what is on the inside? Again, more signs. Our female shopper has a pile of packages now and momentarily is standing on a corner looking a little lost. She has moved near the curb and appears to be looking down the street. Now she is moving again and enters another "stage." The front window of this building is filled with cans of paint. Guess what she comes out with this time?

Each organization resembles a theater stage. Each is located in a specific place and has a particular program of activity. Thus, each has its own *domain*. That is, expectations are communicated to us about the type of activity that goes on there. We don't need to know any of the actors personally. Rather, if we want our shoes repaired, we don't go to the stage with "Golden Arches" where hamburgers are served. Thus, just as many individual actors wear "signs" to help differentiate clerks from other customers, so too participants construct signs to tell us what type of drama takes place within their particular behavior setting. Think how these actors use other types of signs to tell us where their stage begins and ends.

GUARDING THE DOORS

Organizations vary greatly in their degree of openness. Some stages may be entered rather easily like most of the examples we have discussed so far. In contrast, think of a maximum security prison. See how restricted the movement is? And if you think it's hard getting in, try getting out.

We can't just walk into a prison like we do in a paint store. But note: We can't enter the paint store stage anytime either. The drama takes place only at designated times. These times, just like the type of activity that takes place there, are communicated to us so subtly that usually we just take it for granted. Yet, think how such norms guide our behavior and serve to create the patterns we labeled "runabout periods."

Within most organizations, there are areas we may not enter. We easily penetrate the boundary that designates the supermarket stage. But note how the meat counter signals a place to stop. Wearing the uniform of a butcher we might go "back stage" and cut our own meat. Trying to enter without the uniform would probably result in at least an exchange of words. As long as we play our part as customer correctly, we might enter the stage, select our groceries, pay for them, and exit, without necessarily speaking a word. However, deviations, like violating a boundary, must be dealt with. Such an exception, like other types, usually requires verbal exchanges as actors seek to explain the appropriate rules or on occasion, renegotiate them.

Thus, upon looking around within any organization we detect many other types of signs, sometimes written, but often as not, communicated by dress, that designate "back-stage" areas which are accessible only to special actors. Most of us will never enter a hospital surgery room except to play a special part. And when we act the part of a surgical patient, we usually never speak a word, that we are aware of at least. Within organizational stages then, certain areas are often restricted for special players, at special times.

In short, we may enter organizational stages only at specified times and through designated points of entrance. Within these behavior settings, certain areas are restricted to special players who enter and exit at designated times. Bank janitors are expected to enter the executive lunchroom, but not for the purpose of eating lunch. At least not at noon! Such boundary expectations are communicated in many ways ranging from simple written signs (e.g., "Trespassers will be prosecuted") to uniforms (e.g., guards moving throughout a prison); to code words (e.g., Air Force personnel reporting for duty in an underground missile facility); to rings (e.g., identification of fraternity members); and secret gestures (e.g., while socalled intellectuals may look with amusement at the elaborate rituals of greeting used by some fraternal groups, even *Phi Beta Kappa* members are taught a secret handshake upon induction). Thus, organizational stages, both "front" and "back," are specified for us. And depending upon the part we are to play, we learn where to go and what to do once we get there.

While this imagery fits many activity systems, some organizations are not located within a single building or limited geographical area. A bank may have branch offices scattered throughout the city. For reasons distinctive, yet similar in a sense to bank branches, so too are the personnel within the fire department. Perhaps the extreme is represented by the police department whose cruiser operators are constantly on the move throughout the city. Yet there are boundaries for them too. Their activities are guided by boundaries that are invisible and often follow very irregular geographical contours. Customarily, city police attend to activities within their political jurisdiction. Citizens reporting crimes that literally took place across the street may be told to go to another stage. "That's outside our jurisdiction."

Within and without these organizations stages, "jurisdictions" are specified. Participants, on stage within one police department might be able to deal with the reported crime as easily as their counterparts, but an invisible boundary precludes their involvement. Whether they could do the job adequately is not the issue. While it may appear so at first, the example is not unique but rather commonplace. One of us might be able to enter a hospital surgery room and perform an excellent operation. The quality of our work, however, matters not. If we violate the boundary and enact a part for which we are not "certified" we remain an imposter. Whether the patient recovers or dies does not affect the judgment that our behavior was a transgression. And the same is true for organizational representatives. Thus, normative boundaries limit the jurisdiction of local police and F.B.I. agents alike; even the powers of U. S. Presidents are circumscribed.

We've come a long way from our helicopter observation post. Let's quickly review the main points before we move on.

VARIETIES OF INTERACTION SYSTEMS

Our purpose here has been to introduce you to an imagery—a way of thinking about social life. Stop for a few seconds and try to think about the numerous "stages" you have participated on today. What parts did you play?

Now let's get back into our helicopter observation post above the city. Looking down we can see hundreds of separate interaction systems in which persons are participating throughout the day. Each interaction system has a distinctive domain, i.e., a set of expectations that define ranges of behavior that are appropriate for participants. As customers move from one stage to another, from a store to a bank, to a restaurant, we observe that other actors stay in one particular setting throughout the day. About 4:30 P.M., most will start home, fighting their way through streets of traffic.

Tomorrow during the morning "runabout period," most will return to their proper location. And so the pattern of activity is repeated once again.

Despite the regularity of such patterns, these persons are not rats in a maze. Each has his own private motives, ambitions, and purposes. However, none are totally free either; each is constrained by numerous sets of rules which guide their behavior, and thus produce a remarkable degree of structure and pattern when viewed from our helicopter vantage point. This is the critical point, for our personal world is largely confined to participation in small groups. Rarely do we think of ourselves as participants within a community comprised of a multitude of complex activity patterns which exist simultaneously. When told that our behavior, like that of other humans, is highly patterned, our first tendency may be to bristle. We are free to do whatever we want, despite what sociologists say. And you are—more or less, depending upon which stage you are located on and what particular part you are playing.[3]

Think back to the many stages you have entered and exited from this past week—sitting in a lecture, eating breakfast at your dorm, reading in the library, paying a bill at the administration building, and perhaps a rock concert at the student union. As a participant, you played a part on each of

3. Current social scientists use several different theoretical frameworks to guide their analysis. The basic assumptions that are made about "human nature" and social life vary also. The philosophical position on which our framework rests might be labeled "soft-line determinism," i.e., persons are more or less free depending upon characteristics of the social structures in which they are participating at a particular point in time. In contrast, others have adopted highly deterministic views; read B. F. Skinner, *Beyond Freedom and Dignity* (New York: Bantam Books, 1971).

these small stages. Collectively all of these stages, plus several others, comprise a larger social unit—the University. On each separate stage a relatively narrow range of activity was defined as appropriate. You went to the dorm cafeteria for breakfast, not the administration building!

Ranges of appropriate activities are specified for entire organizations as well. Of course, in highly complex ones like universities, the range of expectations, i.e., the domain, is very great. For others, like a tire manufacturing firm, the domain is more narrow as it is for pizza parlors, bowling alleys, book stores, and television stations. Thus, the central task, as it is defined by participants, i.e., some of the expectations that comprise an organization's domain, can be identified. Central tasks are narrowly specified in some organizations, but remain very broad and rather vague in others. However, the great degree of organizational specialization becomes apparent quickly through a brief encounter with the Yellow Pages.

Nearly all of us will spend most of our time as participants on substages that are lodged within large organizations. On each substage, a rather narrow range of activities is specified. Our behavior is constrained by knowledge of what others expect of us. It matters not whether we are in the company cafeteria, the sales office, or the procurement division, the range of tolerable behavior remains rather narrow. It must if we are going to be able to play some parts without even speaking to the other players. Recall the woman cashing her check?

Of course, many of our substages will not approximate this degree of specificity and the impersonality it permits. In contrast to an assembly line, where perhaps human behavior is about as narrowly regulated as is

possible, most of us will participate on stages wherein the norms permit wider ranges of behavior. Within rather wide guidelines a great deal of variation and improvisation may be tolerated, even expected. While our degrees of freedom vary depending upon the substage we happen to be acting on and the particular part we are playing, life in American society—truly an organizational society—is radically different from that experienced by other persons who lived at earlier points in history.

How did it happen? How did this massive network of specialized organizations emerge? Why did it happen? Let's explore these questions briefly before we step inside some organizations to see what makes them tick.

For Further Reading

Blau, Peter M. and Meyer, Marshall W. *Bureaucracy in Modern Society.* 2nd ed. New York: Random House, 1971.

A brief introduction to a "sociological gestalt" on organizational analysis.

Etzioni, Amitai. *Modern Organizations.* Englewood Cliffs, New Jersey: Prentice-Hall, Inc., 1964.

A short and widely read statement which describes the historical origins of large scale organizations, the managerial ideologies used, and a critique of these from a structuralist viewpoint.

Haas, J. Eugene and Drabek, Thomas E. *Complex Organizations: A Sociological Perspective.* New York: The Macmillan Company, 1973.

Major conceptual frameworks currently used, key research strategies, and an innovative view of organizations as outgrowths of stresses and strains are described in a systematic and in-depth manner.

Hall, Richard H. *Organizations: Structure and Process.* Englewood Cliffs, New Jersey: Prentice-Hall, Inc., 1972.

Recent research is summarized on structural features, e.g., size, complexity, formalization, and central processes, e.g., decision-making.

Katz, Daniel and Kahn, Robert L. *The Social Psychology of Organizations*. New York: John Wiley and Sons, Inc., 1966.

This is one of the best initial efforts to apply an "open system" theoretical perspective to organizations and integrate research findings in which the reciprocal impacts of personality and social structure are highlighted.

Leavitt, Harold J., Dill, William R., Eyring, Henry B. *The Organizational World*. New York: Harcourt, Brace and Jovanovich, Inc., 1973.

"Young people, well educated and well motivated, have a large potential for changing complex organizations" (p. xvi), propose these authors, who provide a highly readable introduction to the knowledge necessary to equip those interested.

March, James G. *Handbook of Organizations*. Chicago: Rand McNally, 1965.

In this massive encyclopedic volume experts have summarized research on single topics, e.g., field, laboratory or computer simulation methods, and organizations with different tasks, e.g., prisons, military, hospitals, labor unions, and schools.

Scott, W. Richard. "Theory of Organizations." *Handbook of Modern Sociology*. Chicago: Rand McNally and Company, 1964.

This essay synthesizes several key theoretical problem areas, e.g., groups within organizations, and thereby highlights both previous research and that needed in the future.

Weick, Karl E. *The Social Psychology of Organizing*. Reading, Mass.: Addison-Wesley Press, 1969.

A brief and entertaining analysis of how people get organized—or at least how they try to.

2 | Emergence of Organizational Societies

TODAY, as we have just seen, American metropolitan areas, where the great bulk of our population lives and works, are comprised of thousands of organizations. Each organization can be viewed as a separate and identifiable activity setting wherein participants engage in a relatively narrow range of behaviors. And shoes get made, as do curtains, tires and tables. Gasoline is delivered and sold to enable persons to move from one organization to another as they pick up groceries, go to movies, or perhaps even attend a conference on air pollution. Looking down from our helicopter observation point, shifting abstraction levels really, we can see the validity in characterizing America as a society of organizations.

But America hasn't always been this way. Despite our typical nationalist view of things, complex societies existed long before America did. We emphasize this because too often our students appear to reflect an overly simplistic image of history in which the world begins shortly after World War II!

To understand modern organizational life we need to step back and see the unfolding evolutionary processes whereby some human societies have been transformed into complex networks of large-scale organiza-

tions. However, we should recognize that other modes of social organization characterize hunting and gathering, horticultural, or agrarian societies, in which human beings have lived and, in some instances, continue to do so.[1] Thus in a brief, fast-moving, and necessarily oversimplified manner, let's review the basic roots from which American society originated and the processes of change through which its present structure was attained. Only through a better understanding of such processes can we grasp the complexities of modern organizational life and thereby increase our capacity to evaluate today's social critics. However, we hope that our analysis will not be read as a mere academic exercise. Rather we seek to challenge you to ponder the most important question of all: What kind of society do we want tomorrow?

WEBER ON AUTHORITY

Across the scope of human history, societies have differed markedly, reflecting

1. An excellent summary of differing types of societies at various stages of technological development has been prepared by Gerhard Lenski and Jean Lenski. See *Human Societies: An Introduction to Macrosociology*, 2nd ed. (New York: McGraw Hill Book Company, 1974).

different degrees of technological advancement, population sizes, religious and political ideologies, geographical conditions, and the like. One of the first scholars to systematically examine variations in patterns of societal organization was Max Weber (1864-1920).[2] Reflecting the rigor of German scholarship of his day, Weber compared a wide variety of societies and sought to reveal the interdependencies among their economic, political, religious, and educational structures.[3] Such a comparative method highlights the differing types of organizational structures and varying amounts of organization that characterize any society at a given point in time. As Weber's scholarship revealed, the organizing of persons into specialized activity patterns was not a unique product of the nineteenth century. Clearly, the massive building projects left by civilizations of the past are obvious evidence of organizational skills. Picture the pyramids of Egypt, the aqueducts of Rome, or the Great Wall of China. Think of the thousands of individuals that had to be coordinated to accomplish such feats.

But, Weber argued, while forms of social organization could be identified in such empires that resembled those emergent in Western Europe following the Renaissance, there were important differences. In ancient China, for example, humanistic learning, rather than technical proficiency, qualified officials.[4] Administrative work was not segregated from family concerns or alliances as it increasingly was in German, French, English and American governments, businesses, churches, and schools. And so Weber sought to contrast differences, specify similarities, and by shifting abstraction levels to identify analytic concepts whereby societal variations might be understood.

Foremost among the concepts Weber used in his analyses were power and authority. Both of these concepts remain useful tools in organizational and societal analysis today. Let's examine each and see how Weber used them.

If your professor wants you to do something, tells you what it is, and you proceed to do it, we would infer from your behavior that the professor has power over you. Similarly, we might find you obeying the directives of your father, a police officer or a dormitory assistant. In all organizations, power is differentially distributed. Some persons direct the activities of others.

But why? Why do persons repeatedly engage in behavior patterns wherein some follow the wishes of others? Weber's answer—because some individuals have power over others. Individuals living at the time of Nebuchadnezzar or Ramses II, moved stone, cut hieroglyphs, or what have you, under

2. Weber's major works include: *The Theory of Social and Economic Organization,* trans. by Alexander M. Henderson and Talcott Parsons (New York: The Free Press, 1947); Hans Gerth and C. Wright Mills, eds. *From Max Weber: Essays in Sociology* (New York: Oxford University Press, 1946); and Guenther Roth and Claus Wittich, eds., *Economy and Society,* trans. by Ephraim Fischoff, *et al.,* (New York: The Bedminster Press, 1968).

3. Weber rejected the economic determinism of Marx and sought to demonstrate that religious and political factors also were important. Highlighting interdependencies among various spheres of any society, e.g., how political changes may alter educational structures, has been central in the work of many sociologists.

Brief, but outstanding analyses of total societies and the processes by which they change are: Talcott Parsons, *Societies: Evolutionary and Comparative Perspectives* (Englewood Cliffs, N.J.: Prentice-Hall, Inc., 1966) and Wilbert E. Moore, *Social Change,* 2nd ed. (Englewood Cliffs, N.J.: Prentice-Hall, Inc., 1974).

4. Reinhard Bendix, "Bureaucracy," *The International Encyclopedia of the Social Sciences,* ed. by David L. Sills (New York: The Macmillan Company and The Free Press, 1968), II, p. 207.

the direction of skilled architects because of differential power. Because these power relationships persisted for years, indeed several lifetimes, the combined efforts of thousands of people could be integrated and coordinated, thereby permitting the construction of awe inspiring monuments. However, Weber realized that there is much more to it.

Diaries, verbal accounts, and autobiographies from prisoners, be they captured soldiers, civilians herded into concentration camps, or inmates within maximum security prisons, teach us an important lesson about power. Power is nearly impossible to maintain through physical coercion alone. And thus, throughout history, those holding power have sought some other means to maintain it. But how? How do you go about maintaining power over someone aside from physical force? Weber's answer: One *legitimates* it. That is, the existing power arrangement is presented as the appropriate one. The one that is correct, moral, right, and true.

Power that has been legitimated, granted the definition of being appropriate, becomes less precarious, less unstable. Once legitimated, power relationships are maintained through conceptions of authority, although the threat of physical force may remain in the shadows. While prisoners may flee the first instant a guard turns his back, persons who have been slaves since birth are less likely to run because they know they are slaves. Having been taught to accept their master as master, their behavior reflects a set of invisible bonds. These bonds, which are far more effective than those forged from iron, are the expectations they have learned that tell them who they are and what modes of conduct are appropriate for persons like them. Think of the discom-

fort experienced by many students who flounder and fail when their professors demand that they assume greater responsibility for structuring their educational experiences. Many students who are accustomed to passivity and their teacher's authority find such freedom frightening. Many respond quickly by defining the relationship as totally inappropriate: "Individual projects may be all right for grade school children, but college students are here to learn what the professor knows."

Weber argued that societies not only differed in how power was distributed but also in how it was legitimated. And so he inquired into the nature of legitimation. What are the bases of authority through which power had been legitimated in different societies?

Looking across the span of human history he identified three bases of authority. In some social relationships, power seemed to be legitimated through tradition. As children we are taught to obey our parents. Why should a person who "'plays the part" of mother have power over us? If we are designated to play the part of "her child," she should. But why? Simply because of tradition. Thus, we might be told that "Mothers have always had *the right,* indeed the responsibility, to direct the behavior of their children." But what of our mother's brother, as we would find in the Mesakin or Korongo societies?[5] Why should we do as he wishes? The answer would be the same only the labels would be changed. Such power differentials, legitimated through tradition, *traditional authority* as Weber labeled it, undoubtedly are found in all societies.

5. S. F. Nadel, "Witchcraft in Four African Societies: An Essay in Comparison," *American Anthropologist,* LIV (January-March, 1952), 18-29.

In sharp contrast are patterned relationships that persist among persons because of *charisma*. Throughout human history we can find instances where persons willingly, indeed eagerly, did what they were commanded because of charisma. Spellbound by the skill of an orator, a crowd may become a vigilante party and act to set the world right again. And a man may be hanged, or a college administration building occupied, as persons momentarily surrender their freedom and accept as legitimate the power of their "prophet." Not all such relationships are transitory and short lived. Longer lasting organizations may be created as an emergent political, military, or religious leader seeks to construct a following. Like authority relationships based on tradition, those based largely on charisma could probably be documented in all societies. But in some they are more common than in others. That is the key insight Weber provides us.

Thus, while these two modes of legitimation persist in America today, our society largely reflects a different basis of authority. Weber labeled it *rational-legal* authority. It is legal in the sense that it stems from a set of written rules and rational in that compliance is thought to achieve valued ends.

Rational-legal authority has been documented in many other societies throughout history. Societies like those of ancient China and Rome greatly reflected this mode of organization. However, it was only in such locations as Western Europe and America that societies were emerging wherein this third type of legitimation of power permeated every institutional facet of the society. Not only did persons participate in activities directed toward constructing buildings and bridges, but this rational-legal author-

ity pattern characterized relationships in schools, governmental agencies, churches, and the military. Reflecting this basis of authority, organizations in these societies have become increasingly specialized, with narrowly defined tasks. They have become the types of "stages" we saw previously. Compatible with this general ethic of rationalism and legalism, persons entered these stages not because of who their parents were, but because of skills they had learned. Rational-legal authority is the fundamental mechanism that distinguishes bureaucratic organizations from other forms of social arrangements. Thus, it was societies of bureaucracies, wherein more and more activities would reflect such a mode of authority, rather than charisma or tradition, that were emerging, Weber argued.

Bureaucracies? What can be desirable, or even rational about bureaucracies? Aren't they the epitome of inefficiency, waste, and rigidity? Certainly that is the popular folklore we often hear today. But Weber used this term in a more technical sense. Let's see what he meant by it.

BUREAUCRACIES AS IDEAL TYPES

Reinhard Bendix, a Weberian scholar, tells us that bureaucracy initially referred ". . . to a cloth covering the desks of French government officials in the eighteenth century, the term 'bureau' came to be linked with a suffix signifying rule of government (as in 'aristocracy' or 'democracy'), probably during the struggles against absolutism preceding the French Revolution."[6] Later, as governmental rules became excessively elaborate and complex, critics in many European countries used the term in a de-

6. Bendix, *Encyclopedia of Social Sciences*, p. 206.

rogatory sense. And a new stereotype emerged — bureaucrats — inhuman, expressionless, creatures who were mindless, rule following, cold and insensitive. "The rules are the rules—it's not for me to judge them, that's someone else's job. If you have a complaint, go to office 489-C, and speak to the person at desk 1215W; they deal with cases of this particular type." The term evokes such imagery for many today.

However, Weber meant something else. He used the term as a theoretical tool, apart from such value laden judgments. For him, bureaucracy, referred to a mental construct that he called an "ideal type." It does not exist in reality, but is used to specify a series of critical variables that we can use as a comparative base in contrasting organizations. It is a measurement device of sorts. With it we can order a series of organizations that vary in "degrees of bureaucracy." Some will be more bureaucratic than others; none will be identical with the mental construct. Weber was looking primarily at modern administrative organizations, e.g., governmental bureaus, for which he felt this tool would be more applicable. Presumably, the closer existing administrative organizations approximated the ideal type, the more efficient they were. Whether that would hold for social collectivities directed at other types of tasks, such as education, remained an open question. However, some societies had more organizations that resembled this theoretical construct than others. Thus, it serves as a useful tool in comparative analysis of several societies as well as for studies of a single society over time.

A detailed review of Weber's conceptualization and analysis is beyond our purposes here, but we need to get the gist of his argument so as to use it as a jumping off point

in analyzing American society.[7] Let's look at five basic elements that include the major themes of his ideal type. We'll relate each of these back to the imagery of the theater we developed previously.

First, if behavior patterns by persons are going to approximate the special type of interaction system Weber labeled a bureaucracy, then there must be a set of rules and regulations. Reflecting the legalistic quality of the way in which power is legitimated—recall his label, *rational-legal authority*—persons know how to behave because they know the rules. These rules are not just casual understandings; there is a formality about them. They usually are written down so that everyone is clear about what is expected. When the initial text is interpreted differently as any written document is prone to be, the rules are elaborated with addendums through which future conflicts and disagreements may be averted. Because this formalistic quality is so significant, some theorists use it as a key differentiating criterion. Thus, they separate "formal organizations" from other types of interaction systems for specialized analysis.[8]

Thinking back to our analogy of the theater, these rules, procedures, and regulations are comparable to the script. Specific behavioral expectations are written down. Sometimes this includes even the exact words that are to be used. Recall the last telephone sales "pitch" you encountered? Rule books, policy manuals, advising guidelines, and the like, specify the "standard operating procedures" that *guide* the behaviors of organization participants. Again

7. For details see, Weber, *The Theory of Social and Economic Organization,* especially pp. 328-36.

8. For example, Peter M. Blau and W. Richard Scott, *Formal Organizations* (San Francisco: Chandler Publishing Co., 1962), p. 5.

we emphasize the term "guide." Rules may be *used* by organizational participants to achieve their own ends—a point that many using Weber's conceptualization have not emphasized adequately.

Through these rules, specific jobs or tasks are identified for individuals, groups of individuals, and the entire collectivity. The general purposes, goals, missions, or products of the organization, and subunits within, are specified. And there is a division of labor. Not everyone does the same thing, rather actors have specialized parts with prescribed activity patterns. If those "playing" on the substage of "purchasing office" behave according to the script, then persons on the substage of "production" will have the materials necessary to put together the tables and chairs that persons on another substage will sell, once an unsuspecting individual passes by and begins to play the part of "customer." Modern organizations are characterized by complex divisions of labor.

All of these individuals, each involved in diverse activities, must be coordinated and controlled in some way. What if the right parts can't be obtained by purchasing officials? Who decides what to do? Clearly, a decision made in this office will have ramifications throughout the entire organization. The division of labor creates a condition of interdependency so that actions by persons in one part of the system often have serious consequences for others.

In addition to a division of labor—a horizontal differentiation of tasks—there must be a hierarchical or vertical dimension to permit coordination. When the script becomes problematic, there must be someone "upstairs" to whom the issue can be referred. Some issues may go up "several stairs" before they are resolved. "Passing the buck"

behavior is not a result of personality deficiencies inherent in the actors. Rather, such behavior reflects a necessary process within such complex structures if the separate activities of thousands of individuals are to culminate in automobiles, atomic submarines, or crafts capable of taking men to the moon and back.

This dimension of bureaucracies reflects the rationality aspect of the authority base that Weber saw. Many decisions can not be made by individuals who are playing parts at the bottom level of the structure. They don't have the information to ascertain what the effects of the decision might be elsewhere in the structure. Even with the best of intentions, persons playing such parts could make decisions that would play havoc elsewhere. Buying screws that are 9/116 inches in diameter, instead of 7/116 inches, may appear acceptable to the purchasing agent, especially if they are a few cents cheaper. However, unless such an act is coordinated with many other units, the decision could prove disastrous. By referring such decisions to actors "up the structure," a survey of options and consequences can be made. Thus, the rules specify appropriate jurisdictional areas. Some decisions will be made by the head of the production division, but others must be referred "higher up." Failure to refer a decision up to the next level when it should have been is a serious transgression for any participant in a bureaucracy.

With such rationality built into the structure, efficiency is more apt to occur, even if the persons playing many of the parts are not too bright or even particularly committed to the overall goals of the total organization. As long as someone types the purchase order form accurately and according to the rules, the aircraft can get built. He doesn't need to know the principles of design that led to the decision to use screws of smaller diameter nor does his boss, who now has the responsibility of finding a supplier who can provide the items in sufficient quantity at a designated point in time. If the typist plays the part correctly, he will not even question the decision. It must be right because it was made by persons "higher up." Accustomed to acting this way on a daily basis, perhaps the decision to use the aircraft to bomb cities with names he can't pronounce, will be viewed with equal legitimacy! Recall the words of another good bureaucrat Adolf Eichmann; he claimed he did no wrong; he followed his orders with superb skill.[9]

Eichmann, like all participants in bureaucracies, easily became detached from others because these structures permit individuals to play their parts without knowing each other personally. Remember our example of the woman who was cashing a check? She didn't know the teller personally; nor did she need to. They each knew what behaviors were expected and did not require knowledge of one another's likes or dislikes. Bureaucracies permit the activities of strangers to be coordinated effectively. Persons may work in the same organization, indeed on the same substage for a period of years and remain strangers to one another if they so choose. But as inhuman and undesirable as this may seem at first, think of the freedom it provides. You may not wish to become acquainted with everyone. Thus, not only do such arrangements afford greater efficiency, they greatly extend the limits of personal privacy.

Finally, Weber recognized a most important feature in the organizations that were emerging in Western Europe during the nineteenth century. Rules were developed that created acting parts for persons on a full-time basis. Persons were assigned to their parts depending on their technical competence not kinship. While instances of nepotism may still occur, they remain the exception.

Once assigned, persons returned day after day to play their part. If they played it successfully, that is, according to the rules, they might be told one day to play a new part. After accumulating seniority, they might be promoted. Careers, that is, sequences or chains of "parts" were created. Thus, actors might be shifted from one part to another. Superior performance for one "act" might now be rewarded by assignment to a "bigger part." Of course, the "bigger" the part, the larger the check.

These structures resembled pyramids; more assembly line actors were needed than vice-presidents. Hence, upward mobility within the structure was usually highly competitive at any given level. Thus, in addition to fixed salaries that were uniform for all actors playing similar parts, quality performance was encouraged by the possibility of promotion. Of course, most wouldn't be promoted, so how could their motivation be insured? Longevity of adequate performance was rewarded through a "seniority system" whereby participants were given small wage increments and additional special privileges. Currently, these include such inducements as longer vacation periods, special parking places, choice of assignments and offices, and the like.

If promotion within appears distant, participants in bureaucracies may resign to accept jobs with other organizations which may in effect be promotions. Like delimited

9. Hannah Arendt, *Eichmann in Jerusalem: A Report On the Banality of Evil* (New York: Viking Press, 1963).

spheres of decision making that define jurisdictional limits among divisions and subdivisions, the authority of officials is circumscribed by the organizational boundary. Participants may leave voluntarily. This quality severely restricts the modes of control and heightens the competition among organizations since none can afford to become a "training ground" for others. Superior employees must be retained, rather than lost to competitors. Such procedures and concerns are far removed from other forms of social organization in which individuals, at birth, were destined to assume future jobs, usually those of their parents.

It is no accident that the invention and implementation of highly bureaucratic forms of social organization emerged as the legitimacy of the power of absolutist rulers was being questioned and challenged. Confronted with expanding territories of large populations, many rulers in France, Germany, and England had delegated major authority to royal officials by the seventeenth century and slowly the balance of power shifted more and more into bureaucratic organizations.[10]

Of course, following their war with England, the small band of rebels occupying the eastern seaboard of the North American continent did not concentrate power in a single monarch. And while authority relationships were legitimated by both tradition and charisma, legitimation through rational-legal rule structures had special appeal. Thus, when Weber viewed American society near the end of the nineteenth century, he speculated that the nation was, and would continue to be, a fertile ground for the birth and growth of social collectivities characterized by these five qualities: 1) rules and regulations, 2) division of labor, 3) hierarchical authority structure, 4) impersonal orientation, and 5) careers through which persons move across job assignments as determined by their technical competence. Let's turn our attention now to America and see how it became a society of organizations.

LAND OF THE WEANS

A few years ago Robert Nathan prepared a humorous satirical analysis of life in America.[11] Cast as an anthropological expedition about the year 7000 A.D., Nathan's barbs forever caution us to remain skeptical of interpretations by social scientists regardless of their internal logic. In a slightly altered version, CBS Radio Workshop writers dramatized his account of future scientists who described the deductive reasoning processes whereby they concluded that these primitive people referred to their nation as the land of WE, or the US. Many lived in such major cities as Pound-Laundry (i.e., Washington), n. Yok, and Cha'ago. Pronunciation of "Weans" was confirmed upon the discovery of the "talking disk of Oleans." Across thousands of years, the scientists listened with awe to the recorded message: "Weans ain't gona let theyens tell usens how to run things down here. We all can manage usens own affairs and no damn Yankees from the north is gona tell usens nothin." Later disks permit these brilliant futurists to reconstruct some basic elements of the social organization of the Weans' society. For example, their religion of "rock and roll" was carried forth by their charismatic leader—Evis Priestly.

10. Bendix, *Encyclopedia of Social Sciences*, pp. 208-10.
11. Robert Nathan, *The Weans* (New York: Alfred A. Knopf, 1968).

And so always we must be cautious! But a more pointed signal is in order here. We are using the broadest of brushes to portray a highly complex series of processes and interrelated events in a very personalized and interpretative manner. We will do little more than scratch the surface. But hopefully we will stimulate you to dig more deeply into specific topics, *as you must* if you want to try and grasp the complex layers of organizational networks that comprise American society today.[12]

The Beginnings

By 1776, leaders of the four million or so persons who resided within the United States of America knew much about the abuses and potential threats to individual liberties that unchecked power permitted. In the constitution that finally emerged, governmental powers were defined carefully; divided among several units; and a system of checks and balances was created to prevent any single unit from gaining excessive power. While some persons clustered together in small communities, ninety-five percent were farmers. However, different aspects of social life were clearly differentiated. For example, religion was not a governmental function. Education was not a responsibility of the national government. Such type of differentiation is the first requisite, Eisenstadt proposes, who systematically investigated the societal conditions that appear to be necessary for bureaucracies to develop.[13]

In early America an ethic of individual economic achievement abounded, a distinctive and overpowering "ethos," as Weber called it. "Capitalism existed in China, India, Babylon, in the classic world, and in the Middle Ages. But in all these cases, as we shall see, this particular ethos was lacking."[14] What was this ethos? What comprised it? Weber concluded: "Man is dominated by the making of money, by acquisition as the ultimate purpose of his life."[15] This was the ethos—the distinctively American ethos that Weber labeled "The Spirit of Capitalism."

This economic philosophy, Weber argued, fit well with the basic religious teachings of Protestantism, especially as revealed in the doctrines of John Calvin. One was predestined to be among "the elect" or among those committed to eternal damnation. No one could know what his future was. However, according to Weber's interpretation of Calvin, it was one's duty to consider himself chosen and to resist all doubts to the contrary. Doubts could be resisted most effectively through intense involvement in worldly activities. Accumulated wealth that might result from hard work, shrewdness, and thrift, could be interpreted as a sign that one was among the chosen. "God helps those who help themselves."

Less elegant doctrines had long nurtured the qualities required of good businessmen,

---

12. We have relied heavily on the brief history presented in "United States of America," *Encyclopedia Britannica*, 1972, XXII, 578-743.

Such condensed histories, like single shots moved rapidly through motion picture projectors, can aid us in inferring general trends which too easily get lost when focusing on a few events in great detail. Unless otherwise documented, all dates and statistics were taken from this source or the U.S. Bureau of the Census, *Historical Statistics of the United States, Colonial Times to 1957*, Washington, D. C., 1960.

13. S. N. Eisenstadt, "Bureaucracy, Bureaucratization, and Debureaucratization," *Administrative Science Quarterly*, IV (1959), 302-20.

14. Max Weber, *The Protestant Ethic and The Spirit of Capitalism*, trans. by Talcott Parsons (New York: Charles Scribner's Sons, 1958; originally published in German 1904-5; first English translation, 1930), p. 52.

15. *Ibid.*, p. 53.

as Weber discovered when he confronted writings penned by one of the signers of the Constitution, Benjamin Franklin. "Remember, that *time* is money," Franklin wrote in his *Advice to a Young Tradesman* (1748). And he continued: "Remember, that *credit* is money." "Money can beget money. . . . The more there is of it, the more it produces every turning, so that the profits rise quicker and quicker."[16] And Weber concluded: ". . . all Franklin's moral attitudes are coloured with utilitarianism. Honesty is useful, because it assures credit; so are punctuality, industry, frugality, and that is the reason they are virtues."[17]

Against this backdrop, important variations emerged during the early 1800s. In the North, after the invention of the cotton gin (1793), a few small factories had appeared, while plantation life evolved in the South. New inventions spurred new factories, e.g., vulcanization of rubber, the power loom, and the rotary printing press. Very much an era of every man for himself, legitimated by a Protestant doctrine of individual salvation, to be demonstrated by good works and accumulation of wealth, government too reflected the ideology. "To the victor belong the spoils!" once said William L. Marcy, a leading Jacksonian Democrat. With political patronage as a reward for loyalty, politicians had an important inducement with which to build commitments to their emerging organizations.

By 1850, the proportion of the population who were farmers had declined to 66 percent. Of course, many in the small northern cities were recent immigrants, largely from Ireland and Germany (38 percent and 30 percent, respectively, of the foreign born population in 1860). Seeking escape from the misery of famine and political upheaval, many stayed

near where they got off the ships. Some joined other Americans who were pushing westward in search of new farm lands which were made more productive through steel plows (John Deere, 1837), horse-drawn reapers (Cyrus McCormick, 1834), and similar technologies. Of course, others caught "gold fever" and hopped from spot to spot in the Far West hoping to strike it rich. Regardless of their pursuits, however, they added to a mass migration that was delayed only temporarily by Indians, who in 1862 ". . . were designated as wards of the Bureau of Indian Affairs rather than as 'enemies' . . ."[18] For years the battles had gone on, but now they were intensified. For example, in California alone, during the ten year period between 1849 and 1859, seventy thousand Indians were killed by war and disease.[19] And of the over four million blacks recorded in the 1860 census, the great majority were slaves living in southern states where cotton was king.

The newly emerging life styles in farming communities scattered throughout the midwestern plains, gold mining camps in the west, and in embryonic industrialized cities of the northeast, were a sharp contrast to plantation life in the South. Increasingly, the needs of each group were different, as was reflected in their conflicting views on gold prices, tariffs, and the like. These differences and a host of others created an intense strain or cleavage that forced a redefinition of political power. The legitimacy of established power relationships was being debated, and the rights of

16. *Ibid.*, pp. 48-49; see also p. 192.
17. *Ibid.*, p. 52.
18. Richard M. Burkey, "Race Relations In the United States," *Dictionary of American History* (New York: Charles Scribner's Sons, in press).
19. *Ibid.*

blacks and state governments were asserted with equal force. Recall the definition of authority contained in the "disk of Oleans"? "We all can manage usens own affairs and no damn Yankees from the north is gona tell usens nothin."

Following the rampages of the Civil War, organizational life took on a new quality of expanded size and increased complexity. For example, combining an invention by Elias Howe (1846) with traveling salesmen who offered payments on time installments, Issac Merrit Singer, enabled thousands of families to purchase a treasured device—a sewing machine. What Singer did with sewing machines, Carnegie did with steel, Rockefeller with oil, and Armour with meat packing. These men and others creatively combined basic technologies, money, and organizational skills to design the initial large scale organizations in America. Each quickly gained near total control of their respective specialized facet of the economy.

Some were not happy, however. And they found they were not alone. In 1867, the first organization of farmers was founded called The Grange. Two years later, the same year that the massive continent was tied together through a golden railroad spike at Promontory Point, Utah, the Knights of Labor was formed. Membership increased rapidly, totaling 700,000 sixteen years later. While workers could do little as individuals, in numbers they had strength. And they intended to use it to get what they had come to believe was rightfully theirs; an eight hour work day and higher wages. Their key weapon? The strike—over 1,600 of them in 1886.

Strikes are volatile social events which can easily go awry. As might have been anticipated, police intervention and a bomb brought violent eruption into a noisy Chi-

cago demonstration on May Day, 1886. Laborers had gathered to listen to courage-inducing speeches designed to erase any remaining doubts about the legitimacy of the strike called against the McCormick Harvesting Machine Company. Following the violence of this "Haymarket Riot," as it was labeled, and lesser events elsewhere, public fears of future violence crystallized.

During this same year, the last major Indian conflict took place when the Apaches were defeated. By now ". . . an estimated 1,000,000 Indians had been reduced to around 200,000 and were forced into impoverished reservations under the paternalistic and often corrupt control of the B.I.A."[20] Thus, with the Dawes Act of 1887, future potential violence was contained through the efforts of federal bureaucrats who were to assist the Indians to give up their narrow tribal perspectives, learn to be farmers, and become assimilated into American society. Let the government insure "justice" for all, let hard feelings be ended. Could this same tactic work elsewhere?

For many Americans, mass labor organizations were not the appropriate weapon to constrain the power of rapidly growing industrial monopolies. But what was? Reflecting growing recognition of a common enemy, the railroad monopolies, a temporary coalition of eastern businessmen and western farmers pressured for a new approach. Through passage of the Interstate Commerce Act (1887), Congress declared that some regulation of the railroads was an appropriate responsibility of the Federal government. However, the powers granted the regulatory unit, the Interstate Commerce Commission, were weak and far less effectual than many had hoped. But the noisy

20. *Ibid.*

20

tactics of the Knights of Labor apparently had moved beyond the point of public backing as reflected in their declining membership. As this occurred, however, Samuel Gompers assumed leadership of the American Federation of Labor, a recently created loose federation of local and craft unions. Over the next thirty years, he built this organization into a powerful weapon.

Financing skill to establish credit so that resources could be purchased; knowledge of a basic technological process; and creation of markets to purchase the product, were the essential ingredients of business success. Of course, persons could be hired to build products as total units, but the assembly line mode of organization was far more efficient. This was especially true given the minimal education and skill levels of most laborers, many of whom were recent immigrants. Thus, interchangeability of parts had its parallel in a division of labor among workers.

"What do working men want?" asked the father of scientific management Frederick W. Taylor.[21] "Higher wages!" And what did management want? "Low overhead." But how could you have both simultaneously? Many were willing to work for "reasonable" wages, if only the labor organizers would stop their harangues. And strikes! Where were they in the Protestant ethic?

Against this backdrop we can better understand why Taylor's message was received so widely. For Taylor argued that the way to maximize both high wages and lower overhead was to divide all tasks into a series of minute subtasks. Each individual would be trained to perform a particular task in the most expedient manner possible. If given a quota, and paid extra for performance beyond this, each worker would be able to maximize his own earnings and at the same time give his employer the lowest possible production cost.

And so, following these basic principles of scientific management, new factories were formed. Mergers of existing ones increased the power of managers. The initial pattern of monopoly was constrained by more federal legislation, e.g., Sherman Anti-Trust Act (1890). However, following the earlier pattern of the American Tobacco Company (1890), and the American Sugar Refining Company (1891), "there was a great burst of mergers from 1898 to 1902."[22] Participants within these organizations sharply increased production of basic materials like steel and iron, which in turn were cycled into new industries producing automobiles, phonographs, telephones, electric lights, and hundreds of other new consumer products.

Throughout this period then (1860-1900), many Americans left their farms. Why? For many reasons. Jobs were available, but so were new freedoms and new excitements. A later song writer caught the mood—after they had seen the city, you couldn't keep them down on the farm!

Muckrackers and the Public Response

American cities lacked much at the turn of the century. A new group of reformers exposed many of the deficiencies. Muckrakers, as they were called, wrote of child exploitation, rat infested meats, and a host of other inhumane conditions.

21. Frederick Winslow Taylor, *Scientific Management* (New York: Harper and Row, 1947); three of his essays were published initially in 1895, 1903, and 1911.

22. Gardiner C. Means, "Economic Concentration," in *American Society, Inc.*, ed. by Maurice Zeitlin (Chicago: Markham Publishing Company, 1970), p. 8.

But whose responsibility was this? Again, government appeared to some to be the appropriate instrument. No longer could the older Jacksonian "spoils system" be the model, nor was the political boss an acceptable alternative. Reform government began in larger cities where conditions were worse —Cleveland, Chicago, New York, San Francisco, and other locations where large numbers of families were crowded together. New regulations and a new civil service bureaucracy to oversee them were established. People did not need to be crowded into shacks, so building codes were designated and park systems were created. Police, fire, and sanitation units were initiated in an effort to cope with problems made severe by highly dense population clusters. Municipal ownership, or strict regulation if privately owned, was defined as acceptable for basic utilities like water, gas, and electricity. When population densities changed from 4.4 per square mile (1790 U. S. Census) to that found in such emerging cities, these new types of organizations appeared essential to many.

Another layer of regulation and controls were pushed at the state level by Robert M. LaFollette who served as the governor of Wisconsin at this time (1900-1906). In addition to a state level civil service system, he introduced the first state income tax and implemented numerous state commissions to regulate banking, insurance, and railroad organizations. Many of these reforms like those initiated within particular cities were quickly copied by other states. Thus, in contrast to the initial use of bureaucratic arrangements to produce goods whereby some might become wealthy, and perhaps thereby demonstrate that they were among "the elect" and destined for eternal salvation; new types of problems gave rise to new organizations which were modeled after the basic bureaucratic principles that had worked so effectively in mass production tasks.

However, whether these principles always specified the appropriate organizational form was debated. There were alternatives which reflected the values subscribed to by some. In education, for example, as Michael Katz has documented, many wanted to maintain tight local control of their schools.[23] Others, for mixed reasons, favored private schools, fearing the consequences of centralized education. But, here too bureaucracy won out as the basic organizational mold.

It was about this time that public schools emerged in the minds of many as a tool to maximize a supreme American value—upward social mobility. Of course, they didn't call it that. Rather, not unlike parents in other societies, these new city dwellers from nearby farms, or war ravaged nations across the sea said simply, "I want a better life for my kids than I had." Public education appeared to be the answer. Thus, following the judgments of a newly emerging group of "professional educators," parents protected their children from the dangers of the city, and got them out of the house by sending them to school. Between 1886 and 1910, the average length of school terms was increased sharply from 130 days where it had been for years, to about 157 days.[24] In school most of the day which compulsory attendance laws insured, they could learn the requisites of bureaucratic life: punctual-

23. Michael B. Katz, "From Voluntarism to Bureaucracy in American Education," *Sociology of Education*, (Summer, 1971), 297-332.
24. Abbott L. Ferriss, *Indicators of Trends in American Education* (New York: Russell Sage Foundation, 1969), p. 170.

ity, conformity, and the legitimacy of being judged on their performance.

For many then, the public schools became an agency of escape. Men, and even some women, could flee the poverty of their parents through occupations available only to those with advanced education. Most successful in establishing educational credentials as a basis for restricting others from "playing" their part were physicians. Through their powerful organization, the American Medical Association (founded 1847), they were able to get many states to adopt licensing procedures. But remember, the public did want protection from "quacks," and there were many at this time. Since then, think of how other groups have sought to control the supply of skills available through similar tactics.

Increases in governmental power and organization at the federal level emerged concurrently. Upon the assassination of President McKinley (1901), a man with a different definition of governmental responsibilities stepped into the White House, Teddy Roosevelt. Earlier he had gained quite a public image through organizing a group of "Rough Riders" with whom he fought in Cuba. And now he wasted little time in establishing new precedents for the regulatory powers of the federal government. In less than six months after he was sworn into office, his attorney general announced a suit to dissolve a massive railroad holding company. A few months later when coal miners struck, Roosevelt threatened use of the army to keep the mines open. He averted prolonged conflict and threatened work stoppages by forcing mining operators to meet with him and union representatives whom they consistently had refused to recognize.

This was just a beginning. Following his election to the office (1904), the pace quickened. Under Roosevelt's leadership a host of legislation was passed by Congress which established new organizations with broad domains, for example, Pure Food and Drug Act, requiring the labeling of foods, and a stockyards act, establishing meat inspection. Through the Hepburn Act (1906), the Interstate Commerce Commission finally gained the power needed to regulate railroads more adequately. Recognizing the limits of American forest lands, Roosevelt pushed in an unprecedented manner to create national parks and forests. By the end of Roosevelt's second term, federal spending had reached an all time high ($659,196,000 in 1908 vs. $10,786,000 in 1800). Of course, there had been an increase in population, from 5,297,000 (1800) to 88,709,000 (1908). But this increase was only by a factor of less than seventeen, compared to a factor of sixty-one for federal spending over the 108 years.

Following the more conservative administration of Taft, in 1913, Woodrow Wilson signed into law provisions for a graduated income tax (included in the Underwood Tariff Act) and modernization of the American banking system (Owen-Glass Federal Reserve Bank Act). One year later, more anti-trust legislation was passed through which the Federal Trade Commission was established (Clayton Amendment). And so it continued, as Wilson and his supporters sought to remedy what they defined as injustices through the creation of more federal regulations and organizations, for example, long term loans for farmers (Rural Credits Act, 1916); exclusion of products by child laborers from interstate commerce (Keating-Owen Child Labor Act, 1916);

and an eight-hour work day for interstate railroaders (Adamson Act, 1916).

Recognizing the limitations of state governments to mobilize resources, Wilson succeeded in establishing a mode of assistance for road building and improvement. Thus, use of state grants-in-aid was established through the Federal Highway Act (1916). This pattern of centralization of power at the federal level was accelerated with the onset of World War I during which massive new controls were adopted. And reflecting a pronounced characteristic of Americans—a highly moral orientation, that is, a tendency to judge people and events as right or wrong, good or bad—thousands of "Doughboys" went abroad to "make the world safe for democracy."

Elation and Hangover

By 1920, the war was over and most Americans, half of whom now lived in cities or small towns, yearned for the return to normalcy which Harding promised in his presidential campaign speeches. During the next ten years (1920-1930), more and more of the population, especially the young, were captivated by the excitements and freedoms promised in the city. They learned even earlier now through a new communication device, the radio.

Certainly this innovation aided in the transformation of the Protestant ethic which was occurring. Now, Americans worked hard to buy more and more consumer products. While concern with evidence of being among the "elect" lessened, as Weber saw in Calvinism, the desire to purchase new products intensified as previous luxuries like indoor plumbing and electricity became defined as necessities.

Of course, travel from farms to nearby cities was facilitated through miles of all weather roads. Indeed, reflecting the impact of Wilson's earlier legislation, in just ten years (1917-1927), 74,491 miles of highway were built through combined federal and state monies. Of course, the growing popularity of the automobile was not due to its transportation function alone. Here was a status symbol that everyone passing your house could see at first glance. And as the young quickly discovered, the automobile afforded far more privacy than front porch swings!

These were the Roaring Twenties. And in larger cities the roars were loudest. Reflecting heightened levels of prosperity and shortened hours of work, new developments in recreation and leisure exploded. Ever hear of Babe Ruth? It was during these years that "The Babe" became an American legend as organized baseball emerged as a national pastime. On make-shift sand lots all over the nation, thousands of potential Ruths learned the American values of competitiveness and evaluation based on performance rather than family name or place of birth. For when a fast breaking curve ball catches the corner of the plate, family name matters little. While the route was different, the fame and wealth it promised and the basic values that organized athletics reflected, especially baseball at this time, were highly compatible with those romanticized earlier by Horatio Alger in his stories of "Ragged Dick" and "Tattered Tom." Any man could make it or so the mythology promised.

While many yelled at baseball games, some marched for women's voting rights, and others debated the pros and cons of alcohol. However, most failed to ascertain the transformations that were occurring to the organizations in which they worked; small ones were disappearing rapidly and big ones were growing like raging forest fires. Between 1919 and 1930, "the total number of mergers was about 2,100, five times the number during the period from 1877 to 1904."[25] Thus, modern corporations emerged and grew rapidly. The extent of concentration by 1929, that was documented a few years later by two economists, Berle and Means,[26] remained unknown to most: the 200 largest corporations legally controlled 58 percent of the reported net capital assets of all nonfinancial corporations.[27]

Political scientist, Robert Presthus, suggests that "Mergers occur, apparently, in good times when conservative public opinion eases antipathies toward monopoly and encourages corporations to protect their gains or to spread their risks by merger."[28] And these were good times as Presthus's evidence indicates. "By 1925, the sixteen largest public utilities controlled over fifty percent of the total national generating capacity*. In 1921, the total number of banking establishments was over 30,000; ten years later the number had been reduced by almost one third. At the same time, an urge to expand appeared in other fields such as retailing. The A & P chains, which had some 5,000 stores in 1922, had added 12,500 more by 1928.**[29] And recognizing the potential represented by increased population concentrations, managers of Montgomery Wards and Company and Sears, Roebuck, and Company, decided to augment their massive mail order business by establishing stores in hundreds of American cities. To a lesser degree this same trend characterized public education, as the number of one-room schools decreased, and many professional educators began to argue for the advantages of consolidation.[30]

For the most part, these large organizations were modeled after the bureaucratic principles specified by Weber. Enjoying a material richness that no people in any society had heretofore experienced, it must have seemed to many that the ideal society had finally been created. That many remained poor seemed unimportant. Besides, remember, "God helps those who help themselves." Let them get with it!

Then the bubble popped! Urged to spend and invest and spend more, most did, largely through extending their credit. However, when later confronted with reduced demands, large companies lowered their prices only slightly and began to reduce production. In an earlier era of smaller organizations in intense competition with one another, such conditions might have evoked a response of greatly reduced prices. But layoffs, stemming from production cuts, only further reduced purchasing power and the downward spiral worsened.

While the complex network of forces that culminated in the depression of the thirties, remains debatable even today, we can say that on September 7, 1929, the stock market dropped sharply and continued to do so. By "Black Thursday," seven weeks later, many

25. Robert Presthus, *The Organizational Society* (New York: Vintage Books, 1962), p. 71.
26. Adolf A. Berle, Jr. and Gardiner C. Means, *The Modern Corporation and Private Property* (New York: The Macmillan Company, 1933).
27. Means, *American Society, Inc.*, pp. 2-16.
28. Presthus, *The Organizational Society*, p. 71.
29. *Ibid.*, pp. 71-72. Sources cited by Presthus are: *—Federal Trade Commission, Electric Power Industry, 70th Congress, 1st Sess., Senate Doc. 46, p. 176; **—H. W. Laidler, *Concentration of Control in American Industry* (New York: Thomas Y. Crowell Co., 1931).
30. Ferriss, *Indicators of Trends*, pp. 284-85.

knew that the situation was serious. Of course, President Hoover responded and tried to bring the machinery of the federal government to the rescue. But no one knew exactly where the problem lay and things only worsened. All of the freedom and security that the new life in large-scale organizations had offered, suddenly turned sour. Banks continued to close; unemployment increased; and bread lines formed. Against such odds, faith is hard to retain. "Buddy, can you spare a dime?"

"So, first of all, let me assert my firm belief that the only thing we have to fear is fear itself." So said Franklin Delano Roosevelt when he took office March 4, 1933. In the hundred days that Congress met after his inauguration, the American public was bombarded with a seemingly endless stream of new federal programs dreamed up by the "brain trust," so named because many of his newly appointed advisors were former college professors. And the nation confronted a complex bowl of alphabet soup!

First came the AAA (Agricultural Adjustment Act, through which "parity prices" for farm products were guaranteed in exchange for reduced output), which reflected the pressures of the major farm organizations. Recall the Grange, which we mentioned earlier. Since its founding, farmers had added two other groups: the National Farmers Union (1902), and the American Farm Bureau Federation (1919). Next came the NRA (National Recovery Act) which established committees representing major industries who were charged with designing labor standards and fair practice codes. Under this Act, workers were guaranteed the right to bargain collectively. But the hungry still had to be fed. So the FERA (Federal Emergency Relief Administration) was established to aid state welfare groups. How-

ever, deciding that more drastic action was needed, Congress authorized creation of several federal work programs: the CCC (Civilian Conservation Corps), the CWA (Civil Works Administration) and later the WPA (Works Progress Administration). Farmers and city dwellers alike were assisted through refinancing and new loans on their property as a host of new rules were established by the FCA (Farm Credit Administration), the HOLC (Home Owners' Loan Corporation) and later the FHA (Federal Housing Authority). To bring electricity into homes at controlled and cheaper prices, Roosevelt authorized the massive TVA (Tennessee Valley Authority). Later, even more were aided by the creation of the REA (Rural Electrification Administration). Of even greater impact on all Americans since August, 1935, was the passage of the Social Security Act, which established far-reaching programs for aiding elderly, blind or crippled persons, dependent children and those unemployed.

New Leaders and New Forms of Power

During the same year (1935), the so-called Wagner Act was passed, which finally guaranteed, through federal law, the right of workers to bargain collectively and report "unfair" labor practices to a new federal "watchdog," the NLRB (National Labor Relations Board). Union memberships rocketed upward as men like John L. Lewis, President of the United Mine Workers, pushed hard to capitalize on the mood of the times. With the passage of the Wagner Act, new horizons were possible and the CIO (Congress of Industrial Organizations) was created in an attempt to build vertical structures among all workers within one type of industry. The power of such structures was realized quickly, when General Motors recognized the United Automobile Workers in 1937. Of course, the power struggle was not without violence as many business owners continued to resist unionization with vigor. Power is rarely transferred without a fight and not all of this fighting was done with words or through legally prescribed bureaucratic channels. However, the tide had turned and labor unions became permanent fixtures in the American economy with nine and one-half million members by 1941, over half of which had been gained in just six years.

As the maze of federal organizations began to operate, many had doubts. Despite the enormity of the pain brought by the Depression, this appeared to be too much. Where was America headed? Recall the concerns of the constitutional designers who knew well the dangers inherent in excessively centralized and powerful national governments. If the President and the Congress failed to appreciate their wisdom, that left only the courts. And they responded, declaring several of Roosevelt's programs unconstitutional. Thus, it was no accident that a key issue in the 1936 election was the U. S. Supreme Court and assertions by Alfred M. Landon, the Republican candidate, that if elected, Roosevelt would seek to alter this body—the sole check on his power. Upon his election, stressing that the ends justified his action, Roosevelt did just that. ". . . I see one-third of a nation ill-housed, ill-clad, ill-nourished." The nation watched as an intense power struggle unfolded. Should persons who were over seventy be replaced on the court, or at least be rivaled by new Presidential appointees? But here Roosevelt was stopped.

While Americans debated, new leaders emerged elsewhere in countries that lacked the organizational machinery to curb their powers. First, Mussolini's troops invaded Ethiopia (1935). Then the Japanese military began moving into China (1937). And two years later, under the direction of Adolf Hitler, thousands of German soldiers invaded Poland. To most Americans, however, entanglement in one war abroad in a lifetime was enough. Reminiscent of Landon's previous warnings, many listened with concern as Wendell Willkie charged that Roosevelt would carry the United States into war; but Roosevelt won again. Despite their defeat in the 1940 election, isolationists continued their battle and organized behind their own charismatic leader, Charles A. Lindbergh. They remained undaunted by the coalition pact which united Germany, Italy and Japan (1940).

The debate was soon settled, however, with the bombing of Pearl Harbor, December 7, 1941. Once again, war brought increased powers to the federal government as attention was focused on a common enemy; massive new federal organizations were created to insure his defeat. Participants in them oversaw the distribution of the nation's resources among thousands of factories that were quickly converted into military suppliers. Given the rich natural resources available and the organizational skills of manufacturers who earlier had designed systems to absorb poorly educated European immigrants, but now had to adapt to a new labor base comprised largely of women, an unprecedented volume of tanks, ships, airplanes, and weapons of all kinds flooded out. By 1944, U. S. war production was twice that of the three axis powers combined.

But this war, reflecting recent technological and scientific discoveries, required more. Specialists were organized and hidden away in top secret laboratories, many of which were located in desolate areas like Los Alamos, New Mexico. It was near here at a place called Alamogordo that it happened. On July 16, 1945, the human race entered a new era with an explosion that signaled man's creation of a totally new type of power—atomic energy.

A less visible new type of power had emerged elsewhere and had made its initial appearance the year before, when Thomas E. Dewey was defeated by Roosevelt, in part through the efforts of the CIO. Dewey's unexpected defeat four years later, by a rough-talking, hard-punching Democrat from Missouri, Harry S. Truman, was further evidence that organized labor was a force that would have to be reckoned with. Thus, by now the precarious balance among four "countervailing powers," as John Kenneth Galbraith labeled them later, had been established: vertical structures, controlled by business interests now rivaled by a powerful federal bureaucracy, networks of labor unions and three massive farm organizations.[31]

More Foreign Entanglements

Contrasting the strong isolationist mood of the late 30s, the war's end brought a whole new layer of organizational networks—the United Nations organization was created (1945). Recovery abroad was coordinated through the "Marshall Plan" as President Truman sought to grasp the host of organizations that now confronted him. And so, with massive outlays of American dollars, Europe, Nationalist China and Japan were rebuilt with the hope that a more enduring stability might be attained that would curb the rising threat of Communism.

At home, Truman signed bills to deal with new problems that resulted from actions taken during the war. For example, to control the awesome power represented by the knowledge of nuclear fission, and to insure American supremacy, the AEC (Atomic Energy Commission) was created. Similarly, to reduce the infighting among the various armed forces, and to coordinate their post-war dismantling, the DOD (Department of Defense) was established. Under the rhetoric of a "Fair Deal," Truman authorized additional federal spending in hopes of easing the post-war readjustments of many Americans who now wanted to resume their family life. Through federal assistance, many secured loans to establish new businesses, while thousands more extended their education through the "G.I. Bill of Rights" and purchased new homes with low interest "G.I. loans." Thus, life in suburbia was created; that is, if you were white. For while whites began a massive exodus into suburbia, blacks began pouring into the central cities. Places like Cleveland, Chicago and Los Angeles were transformed in a decade. But within suburbia and the core cities one sound was common—the cry of newborn babies. Thousands of them! And they created a major bulge in the U.S. population pyramid.

Conflicts continued. At home, many in Congress feared the increasing power represented by organized labor. They responded with new legislation finally enacted over Truman's veto, the Taft-Hartley Labor Management Relations Act (1947). And while a senator from Wisconsin, Joseph McCarthy, looked for Communists within

31. John Kenneth Galbraith, *American Capitalism: The Concept of Countervailing Power*, (Rev. ed.; Boston: Houghton Mifflin Company, 1956); see especially pp. 108-65.

the federal government, the Soviet Union aided troops that on June 25, 1950, pushed across the 38th parallel into the tiny country of South Korea. Once again, this time under the auspices of the fledgling U.N. organization, Americans were fighting abroad. Still most failed to recognize the threat that the Soviet Union represented. Churchill's words seemed like so much poetry as treaties were signed in 1952 that granted the U.S.S.R. control of territory it occupied at the end of World War II—an Iron Curtain? Come now!

Fighting in Korea intensified, and many wanted the U.S. out of it. "Why were we there anyway?" "Who was to blame?" Pointing his finger directly at Truman, General Dwight D. Eisenhower—Ike, as he had come to be known by most during the previous war—appeared to a majority of Americans to be a favored choice over the difficult-to-comprehend "egghead" from Illinois, Adlai E. Stevenson. Ike had promised he would go to Korea, and he did.

The Web of Interdependency Tightens

During his term as President, Eisenhower sensed that the linkages among business and government, especially the military, were tightening. Reflecting this perception, he confronted Americans with a new term called the military-industrial complex, in his farewell address (January 17, 1961). The concept remained rather meaningless to most people. However, some of his actions generated more immediate response, such as his appointment of Earl Warren as Chief Justice of the U. S. Supreme Court. Conservatives intensified their attacks following the 1954 desegregation decision (Brown vs. Board of Education of Topeka, Kansas) in which Warren declared that the previous

policy set in 1896 that permitted "separate but equal" schools would stand no longer. It was the responsibility of the federal government to enforce the Constitution and that meant that public school segregation had to end. The implications of this decision remained vague to most, especially whites living in new suburban homes in Northeastern, midwestern and western cities which were now experiencing a new process called metropolitanization. Even less clear were the terms through which troops located in Korea had come home. Despite these ambiguities, and a serious heart attack in 1955, Eisenhower defeated Stevenson in 1956.

One year later, a shocked nation appeared unable to comprehend that its supremacy in science and technology was being questioned. How could the U.S.S.R. have accomplished the impossible? Sputnik precipitated large scale appraisals. Many charged that the schools were at fault. But direct federal intervention here was impossible, since education was clearly and solely a state responsibility. The pressure for reform and experimentation intensified.

By this time, the push for Negro civil rights was gaining a head of steam. Some avenues, like organized athletics, made upward mobility possible for a select few. A handful of heroes had emerged earlier, like Joe Louis in boxing. But as Jackie Robinson penetrated the boundary of major league baseball, heightened levels of involvement were demanded in all institutional facets of American society. Living abroad during World War II and Korea made accepting home impossible for many.

In contrast to athletes, the Montgomery, Alabama, bus boycott uncovered a different type of charismatic black man, Martin Luther King, Jr. And blacks, be they Mrs. Rosa Parks, or anyone else, were no longer willing to sit only at the back of the bus. "Nonviolent resistance," King called it, and the legitimacy of many local laws was challenged. To some this appeared as reckless lawlessness. But others recalled the earlier words of Henry David Thoreau who also recognized that unjust laws may exist. When so judged by one's conscience, civil disobedience, with full acceptance of the consequences, may be in order.[32] To do otherwise is to accept the position of Adolf Eichmann.

In the Warren decision (1954), the U.S. Supreme Court had made it clear that segregation of the public schools was illegal, whether those schools were located in California, Wyoming, or Arkansas. Once again, the jurisdictional authority of states was challenged. Like previous Presidents confronted with defiance of the law, Eisenhower had little choice but to send troops to Little Rock, Arkansas, and thereby insure that the constitutional rights of black children would not be violated.

Through victories like these a sense of momentum was gained, as blacks, who were often joined by whites, continued to press for an end to the injustices of three hundred years. Thus, in the 1960s, hundreds of "freedom riders" invaded southern communities in an effort to dramatize a reality that most Americans wished to repress. Repression was difficult given the powerful medium of television as reporters from the three national networks competed to capture history in the making. As you should anticipate by now, several new organizations were created to maximize these efforts, e.g., CORE (Congress of Racial Equality) and SNCC (Student Nonviolent Coordinating Committee).

While many of these actions remained highly controversial, it was clear that thou-

sands of Americans were sympathetic with the ends, if not the means, towards which they were directed. Then, while Martin Luther King, Jr., sat in a Georgia jail and sought words with which to communicate his dream for America, one presidential candidate—a rich, young, Irish, Catholic from Boston, announced his admiration for King. Certainly without the Negro vote, John F. Kennedy would have never squeaked by Eisenhower's former vice-president, Richard M. Nixon. And equally certain, television played no small part in this election, either.

Kennedy had many plans to mobilize the federal bureaucracy. His rhetoric of "the new frontier" captivated many of the young. But many congressmen, especially southern democrats, were less impressed and most effective at applying "legislative brakes." Then, and the impact was heightened by television, the fourth American president was killed by an assassin. And into the White House stepped Lyndon B. Johnson, longtime senator from Texas. The national mood was intense; what better way to pay tribute to a courageous president than to unclog the log jam. In a flurry of congressional activity, reminiscent of his mentor F. D. R., Johnson pushed into law numerous acts, most notably the 1964 Civil Rights Act, which was filibustered in the Senate for three months, and the Economic Opportunity Act, a broad "antipoverty" bill.

However, fearing an increasingly powerful bureaucracy, many campaigned hard for "Mr. Conservative," Senator Barry Goldwater, who preached a doctrine of American self-determination, with less interfer-

32. Henry David Thoreau, *Walden and On the Duty of Civil Disobedience* (New York: New American Library of World Literature, Inc., 1956; original publication, 1854 and 1849).

ence from Washington bureaucrats. Only six states—Arizona, Goldwater's home state, and five deep southern states—went for his views, however, as Johnson won by a landslide in 1964. With this mandate, the tall Texan began his own legislative program, designed, he claimed, to bring into being within the next decade the "Great Society." Thus, for the first time, American schools vibrated upon receipt of the massive shot of adrenaline provided through the 1965 Education Act. Johnson appointed numerous "task forces" who quickly responded with elaborate recommendations whereby everything from crime to air pollution could be remedied. To alter the pattern of deterioration of the central cities, which were becoming increasingly populated by blacks and other minority peoples, Johnson declared "war on poverty" and pushed through Congress numerous bills designed to assist local governments to cope with mounting problems.

But the summers of 1964, '65, and '66 were hot! Aspirations had been raised and the powder keg conditions that earlier observers had noted (e.g., James B. Connant, *Slums and Suburbs*, New York: McGraw-Hill Book Company, 1961) could no longer be contained. In city after city, local police sought to squelch violent rampages that the news media rapidly publicized under the label of "ghetto riots." "Between 1964 and 1968, there were 239 cases of hostile black protest and outbursts in 215 cities, lasting 523 days, involving 49,607 arrests, 7,942 wounded and 191 deaths."[33]

While these battles escalated, Johnson confronted intensification of conflict throughout Indo-China, most notably in the small nation of South Viet Nam. Through treaties with this government, American authority too, was being challenged. When so challenged, the threat of physical coercion that normally hides in the shadows must be unveiled. And Johnson did just that with a massive show of strength.

But instead of pulling the country together, as many previous military conflicts had done, this one ripped the nation apart worse than any period since the Civil War. Across the country anti-war groups mobilized, slowly at first, but with increasing strength. Assassinations of Martin Luther King, Jr. and Robert Kennedy, only stressed further structures that were already highly strained.

The Bulge Speaks

Against these conditions, a small majority sided with Richard Nixon's campaign rhetoric that urged Americans to turn down their voices and let those with calmer dispositions prevail. However, in May, 1970, when he announced that U.S. troops had invaded Cambodia, masses of war protestors were shocked. While the American public had witnessed via television the violence of a jungle war and conflicts in the ghettos, many—especially the college aged—could not accept the legitimacy of any authority that condoned the killings at Kent State University. The bulge in the population pyramid that had created the elementary school crisis at the time of Sputnik with which Eisenhower had to cope, had now reached late adolescence. Among those on college campuses, a sizable segment experienced a temporary radicalization that demanded immediate action. College administrators managed to keep their institutions running more or less. With the coming of summer, as the noise faded away, many

33. Burkey, *Dictionary of American History*.

began to wonder what it all meant. Why were so many of these youngsters who were among the most materially wealthy children in human history so vocally "anti-establishment"? What had happened to the Protestant ethic of which Weber had written?

President Nixon's will prevailed, however. Slowly, U. S. troops began to return home. A sense of calmness and order returned. For many a renewed sense of patriotism was stimulated as Neil Armstrong set his feet firmly on the moon. Here was evidence of organizational skill that boggled the minds of most.

Despite the presence of some U. S. troops in Viet Nam, this issue was largely resolved by 1972, when George McGovern was defeated by President Nixon by even a larger landslide than Johnson's victory over Goldwater. As President, Richard M. Nixon has attempted to reduce the scope and size of the federal bureaucracy. Through a "revenue-sharing" concept he seeks a "New Federalism" wherein state governments will be elevated in power and stimulated to devise their own solutions to their local problems without the constraints of federal approval. Whether this attempt to transfer power to state level government will be accepted over the long run or not will remain problematic for many years.

However, confronted with continuing inflation and serious ecological imbalances, Nixon simultaneously created tough new agencies, e.g., the Cost of Living Council, Price and Wage Commissions, and the Environmental Protection Agency, to further constrain the actions of organizational officials. Industrial wastes, like air pollution, can no longer be viewed as a private problem. The web of interdependency has become too tight.

In compliance with civil rights legislation, however, many Americans remain puzzled by the forced creation of Equal Opportunity offices. Many are even more perplexed as they drive to work past lines of orange and black buses, which, in part, reflect not the decisions of local boards, but of federal judges. Due to the population shifts that occurred through the metropolitanization process of the 1950s and 1960s wherein whites moved to suburbia to enjoy both the richness of the city and a touch of ruralness, racial integration of public schools is simply not possible without transporting some students beyond their neighborhoods and in some cases, e.g., Richmond, Virginia, beyond the limits of their local school districts. Such layers of authority are hard for many to grasp.

This then is a brief and highly incomplete history of the people of "WE" who have discovered, perhaps only temporarily, how to design an affluent society wherein a moderate level of material abundance is distributed broadly. Their organizational structures slowly emerged as individuals who temporarily occupied positions of power sought to use these weapons to expand their sphere of autonomy, degree of security and level of prestige. And so more and more structures were created as persons struggled to advance their causes; erect constraints to limit the power of others; and to insure the survival of their organization in the future. As the web of interdependency tightened, layers of governmental constraints were erected to limit the powers of organizational officials whose actions were increasingly recognized to have impacts far beyond their assumed organizational boundary.

Most American adults are *employees* for large organizations, be they governmental, industrial, communications, finance, retail, educational, or even agricultural. Some evidence suggests that through mergers of many types—be it stronger professional organizations among school teachers or extended control through industrial "conglomerates" which expanded greatly in the past twenty years—power has become more concentrated as the web of interdependence has tightened even more. This is reflected in overlapping directors and mergers. For example; "Among 16 recent directors of United States Steel Corporation, one could account for 20 directorships in major industrials, 18 in banks, 11 in insurance companies, 9 in railroads, 8 in utilities, and 3 in foundations (and 5 trusteeships in universities)."[34] One study found that among seventy-four large firms, 1,480 directors and managers held 4,428 positions.[35] And of mergers—they ". . . increased until 1965 at an annual rate of 3 percent. But from 1965 to 1968 the annual rate of merger had risen to 34 percent, . . ."[36]

Thus decisions made by persons near the top of DOD, GM, ITT, or the like, have rapid and grave consequences for participants in a multitude of parallel structures located throughout the country, and, at times, throughout the entire planet. While many seek to grasp the complexities of these massive organizational networks so that wastage, conflict, and unintentional pain can be minimized, others, who are more disenchanted, suggest that the costs, namely the necessary limitations placed on human freedom, are not worth the benefits, which they see solely as materialistic.

DO NOT FOLD, BEND, SPINDLE, OR MUTILATE

Criticism of organized life in America is not new. Indeed, not liking what he saw in the mid 1800s, Thoreau temporarily with-

drew into the Massachusetts woods to think things over: "It lives too fast. Men think that it is essential that the *Nation* have commerce, and export ice, and talk through a telegraph, and ride thirty miles an hour, without a doubt, whether *they* do or not; but whether we should live like baboons or like men, is a little uncertain."[37] "Men say that a stitch in time saves nine, and so they take a thousand stitches to-day to save nine to-morrow. As for work, we haven't any of any consequence. We have Saint Vitus' dance, and cannot possibly keep our heads still."[38] And what would he say today!

Despite Thoreau and others like him, most Americans believed in the values we have discussed thus far, e.g., materialism, individual achievement, and social mobility or "success," as it was usually called. While there were exceptions, the work ethic prevailed. But having money to buy material possessions was only part of it. Many, not unlike those before them, sincerely desired a more rewarding life for their children. Thus, a central theme of "the American Dream" was to see one's children experiencing upward mobility. "I've scrubbed floors for ten years, but my boy is going to college." And college attendance, like education generally, became increasingly important in the market place, especially after World War II.

34. Charles H. Anderson, *Toward A New Sociology: A Critical View* (Homewood, Illinois: The Dorsey Press, 1971), p. 184.
35. *Ibid.* Study cited is H. L. Nieburg, *In the Name of Science* (Chicago: Quadrangle Books, 1966), p. 196.
36. *Ibid.* Source cited is U. S. Bureau of the Census, *Statistical Abstract of the United States; 1969* (Washington, D. C.: Government Printing Office, 1969), pp. xiii-xvii.
37. Thoreau, *Walden*, p. 67.
38. *Ibid.*

Upon recovering from the explosion created in large part by returning G.I.'s, college administrators now faced rapidly declining enrollments. This was offset, to a degree, by an increased proportion of high school graduates attending, many of whom had been told that a college degree would insure a future, high-paying job, i.e., success. Thus, increasingly for middle-class families—many of whom knew the reality of the depression of the 30s and the uncertainties of lower class existence before that—college attendance was defined as a "necessity" for their children. How better to insure their success?

Following World War II, new voices emerged that were highly pessimistic. While many Americans heard them in one way or another, it was among college students during the 1950s that the works of such writers as Sarte, Camus, Orwell, and Huxley had special appeal.[39] As they read *On The Beach*,[40] fears of nuclear holocaust lead to more intense questioning. "Surely, there must be more to life than the exhausting competitiveness of the market place. But what?" Existentialism became a fad, but still most took jobs upon leaving college.

However, the questioning intensified. Was there no escape from "The Lonely Crowd"?[41] To succeed did one have to become an "other directed" person whose long antenna would always tell you what the group was thinking? The rage grew more intense as hundreds pondered the implications of the analysis by an editor of *Fortune*. In *The Organization Man*,[42] William H. Whyte, Jr., held up a mirror and "conformity" became a dirty word for many as they bristled at Whyte's conclusion: "Once people liked to think, at least, that they were in control of their destinies, but few of the younger organization people cherish

such notions. Most see themselves as objects more acted upon than acting—and their future, therefore, determined as much by the system as by themselves."[43]

But if "the system" was overpowering what did that mean for human freedom? Against this backdrop and the inflated bulge in the population pyramid that brought so many adolescents to colleges all at once, we can better understand why the Berkeley student revolt (1964) gradually became symbolic. And when a former Harvard professor made his pilgrimage across the nation, urging students to "tune in, turn on, and drop out," many found his message overpowering and the hippie appeared. Feeling powerless, yet concentrated on campuses often overly populated by nonteaching professors who were scrambling madly after federal grants, many students experienced intense alienation.[44] Of such stuff is revolution made. Some lashed out and created meaning through intense political actions. Once organized, they set out to conquer dragons—but many of these turned

39. For example, Jean-Paul Sarte, *Nausea* (Norfolk, Conn.: New Direction Books, 1959); Albert Camus, *The Stranger*, trans. by Stuart Gilbert (New York: Alfred A. Knopf, 1946); George Orwell, *Nineteen Eighty-four* (New York: Harcourt, Brace, 1949); and Aldous Huxley, *Brave New World* (New York: Bantam Books, 1958; originally published, 1932) and *Brave New World Revisited* (New York: Harper and Brothers, 1958).
40. Nevil Shute, *On The Beach* (New York: New American Library of World Literature, Inc., 1957).
41. David Riesman, Nathan Glazer, and Revel Denney, *The Lonely Crowd* (New York: Doubleday and Company, 1950).
42. William H. Whyte, Jr., *The Organization Man* (New York: Doubleday and Company, 1957).
43. *Ibid.*, p. 437.
44. See, for example, Kenneth Keniston, *The Uncommitted: Alienated Youth in American Society* (New York: Harcourt, Brace, and World, 1960) and Paul Knott, *Student Activism* (Dubuque, Iowa: William C. Brown, 1971).

out to be windmills. Most attractive among the campaigns, as we noted earlier, was the Indo-China war.

Many others, even before reaching college age, simply dropped out, physically, mentally, or both. They retreated into an underground culture that preached not only tolerance of many mood altering drugs, but emphasized even more the importance of human relationships characterized by a sense of warmth, intimacy, and gentleness. To many over thirty, it was as if they felt that they, the very first in human history, had discovered L-O-V-E. Thus, despite the excesses, exploitations of various types and occasional violence, "hippies" did not go away.

Why? Partially because merchants were quick to exploit the theme through clothes, jewelry, furniture, and especially records, tapes, and musical instruments. The "youth market" was a rich one. But, according to some analysts of American society, the impact was intense because "hippies" had much to say about some critical areas of strain in American society. Fred Davis, for example, suggests that "hippies" are seeking life styles that are not dependent on "compulsive consumption."[45] How much of the "material glut" found in most retail stores is really necessary? Upon close examination, what material items are of absolute necessity? If a frantic competitive and exhausting "rat race" existence is required to purchase such items, why bother? Why not a simpler existence with more time to do what one wants?

"Doing one's thing" emerged as a direct attack on the "passive spectatorship" of middle class America who increasingly occupied their leisure hours by watching professionals be it football, golf, fishing, bowling, or piano. The behavior pattern started early in school with organized athletics. As the years progressed, the proportion of players decreased with a commensurate increase in watchers. Davis articulates the hippie manifesto as ". . . all men are artists—who cares that some are better at it than others, all can have fun."[46]

But when is there time to have fun? "Hard work now will get you better grades. Without them you'll never get into college. And hard work in college will get you a good job that pays well. Stay at it for just twenty years after that and think what you'll have." "Yea, but then what?" The plight of Benjamin, the graduate, became a nightmare for many.[47] And so, rejecting prolonged delays in gratification, Davis suggests that the hippie subculture proposes a revised time scale of experience. Appointments, parcelling out the day into small segments, lists of things to get done, and the like are distained —"Let's hang loose." Reminiscent of Thoreau's earlier plea, many today vibrate to modern day versions expressed in song, e.g., "Slow down, you move too fast, you've got to make the morning last."

How does this philosophy fit into a society of organizations? The clashes are obvious. Thus, some propose that these views are necessarily destined to be short lived. Others, with equal fervor, talk of societal revolution: "the commune will be the basic organizational unit in the society of tomor-

45. Fred Davis, *On Youth Subcultures: The Hippie Variant* (New York: General Learning Press, 1971) and "Why All of Us May Be Hippies Someday," *Transaction*, IV (December, 1967), 10-18.
46. Davis, *On Youth Subcultures: The Hippie Variant*, p. 17.
47. Undoubtedly Charles Webb's novel had it's greatest impact through the movie version; *The Graduate* (New York: New American Library, Inc., 1963).

row." Rejecting both extremes, Davis proposes a trifurcated society. Organizational life will continue for most, but many will "drop out" for a few years. Comprised largely of late adolescents, this "drop-out" segment will recruit some at all age levels. Some will remain longer than others, but most will return to the "straight world" eventually. Finally, he sees a third component that will remain culturally separate—a third world segment comprised mainly of blacks, Chicanos and American Indians. Some in this group may "pass" to varying degrees, but many will seek to retain ethnic pride and identity. Perhaps capturing the great white whale, i.e., middle class materialistic life made possible by large scale organizations, does not represent nirvana after all. Davis' speculations are challenging. Think about them, and ask yourself where is American society headed? What "parts" do I want to "play"?

We believe that large scale organizations are here to stay, at least long after your life has ended. But life in such organizations need not be as inhuman as it is often depicted, or as it often is in reality. We'll return to this theme in our final chapter, but before that argument can be developed, we need to gain a better understanding of how organizations function.

For Further Reading

Bendix, Reinhard. "Bureaucracy." *International Encyclopedia of the Social Sciences.* Edited by David L. Sills. New York: The Macmillan Company and The Free Press, 1968.

A brief historical description of the rise of bureaucracy as a mode of government.

Boulding, Kenneth E. *The Organizational Revolution.* Chicago: Quadrangle Books, 1968.

Case studies of the rise of large organizations, in business, labor, agriculture and government and an assessment of the ethics of such.

Eisenstadt, S. N. *The Political System of Empires: The Rise and Fall of the Historical Bureaucratic Societies.* New York: Free Press of Glencoe, 1963.

Analytical examination of numerous historical bureaucratic societies, e.g., Byzantine and Roman empires, Mogul Europe, the Sung Dynasty, and the processes of change within them, especially their political structures.

Lenski, Gerhard, and Lenski, Jean. *Human Societies: An Introduction to Macrosociology.* New York: McGraw Hill Book Company, 1974.

Couched in an evolutionary theoretical framework, the social organization of societies at varied degrees of technological development is described.

Presthus, Robert. *The Organizational Society.* New York: Vintage Books, 1962.

The transformation of America into an organizational society is traced and the impact of such structures on participants of varied personality types is analyzed.

Roszak, Theodore. *The Making of a Counter Culture.* Garden City, New York: Anchor Books, Doubleday and Company, Inc., 1968.

From Freud and Marx, to Marcuse, Brown and Goodman, to Ginsberg and Watts, the spokesmen are summarized, contrasted, and woven into an historical interpretation of the rise of opposition to American technocracy.

Weber, Max. *The Protestant Ethic and the Spirit of Capitalism.* Translated by Talcott Parsons. New York: Charles Scribner's Sons, 1958 (original German publication, 1904-05.).

Rejecting the economic determinism of Marx, Weber sought to demonstrate the psychological motivations that were rooted in the religious and moral values of American society that made possible the emergence of a capitalistic economic system.

Williams, Robin M., Jr. *American Society: A Sociological Interpretation.* 3rd ed. New York: Alfred A. Knopf, 1970.

A detailed description of the major institutional sectors of American society, its underlying values, and strains among them.

Zeitlin, Maurice. *American Society, Inc.* Chicago: Markham Publishing Company, 1970.

A collection of materials that demonstrate the concentration of wealth and power in America and the logical consequences of poverty and conflict.

3 | Looking Inside an Organization

UPON reading our brief presentation of the historical events and evolutionary processes whereby America was transformed from a loose network of colonies, family farms, and plantations into densely populated metropolitan areas, we can begin to grasp why an understanding of organizations is important if we wish to ponder our own future. Large-scale organizations, wherein most of us living at this point in human history will spend a great portion of our lives, did not appear magically through the waving of a wand by either a savior or a demon. Rather they emerged over time as hundreds of individuals sought to solve diverse problems. For many, the primary concerns were highly localized, maybe even selfish, e.g., financial gains for self or family. Such individuals were constrained by others who discovered gradually that effective weapons could be molded through similar organizational principles. Thus, no organization ever exists in a vacuum; all are enveloped in a network that limits their autonomy or freedom of action. We'll pursue the implications of several types of external tensions and conflicts in an upcoming chapter, but now let's momentarily blot out environmental constraints and look inward.

Do you recall the imagery we developed in Chapter I? Mentally we positioned ourselves in a helicopter above a city, and looking down we saw persons situated within behavior settings. In fact, the city resembled a network of theater stages. Some persons return day after day to play a particular part on a particular stage during specified times. Even the movements of some across the stages assumes a remarkable degree of patterning when viewed from this vantage point.

Description of such behavior patterns is the first step. But note, in taking this step we are creating an object of study. We are assuming that it will prove useful to view the behavior of individuals, each of whom is assumed to have private purposes, motivations, and intentions, in this collective fashion. Why? Simply because we are further assuming that the primary explanation of this behavior will not be found through analysis of individual characteristics, be they psychological variables like intelligence, or biological ones like chromosome composition. This is not to say that these are unimportant. These types of variables establish limits for large-scale behavior patterns among persons. But we believe that the primary explanation will be found at another level of analysis. Pattern and structure emerges in human behavior largely because persons are guided by symbols. Thus, through analyses of symbolizing processes and structural variations in symbolic systems, we can understand the mechanisms through which human behavior patterns emerge, persist and change.

Now let's try it. Let's go inside an organization and explore a few of the concepts sociologists have invented to try and understand these complex networks of human interaction.

BEING A CUSTOMER

Let's start outside; that is, outside of one organizational boundary. Picture yourself sitting in a motel room with your family. You are on a summer vacation and after driving all day you decide to stop in a small city for the night. After a swim and a short rest, thoughts turn toward dinner. Your family has never been in this city before. Since you skimped last night and only snacked in the car throughout the day, everyone is hungry. How can you find a restaurant? Or, returning to our earlier imagery, how can you find a behavior setting—a stage—which you can enter and play the part of customer?

Of course, there are many strategies. You might ask the desk clerk at the motel office. "Oh, our restaurant here is excellent. We are open twenty-four hours too." As an organizational representative, she plays the part well. As a human being, she may even believe it. But what if she didn't? How long could she retain her involvement if she replied everytime: "Oh, gad, don't eat here. The food is putrid. You wouldn't believe the filth in the kitchen. The state health department is trying to close them down."

But what if the food is bad, and yet the desk clerk is directed to try and push the restaurant? What then? While they take many forms, such conflicts are not unusual. Thus, at the start, let's recognize that the behavior patterns we are observing are not those of rats in a maze, nor are they those of theater actors who are merely following a script. Rather, we are observing human beings who have feelings and judgments of their own. They are guided by organizational dictates, but only to a point. The scripts are too incomplete, and all too often they are inconsistent either internally or with scripts from other stages. While we play any one part on a given stage, we also are guided in enacting that part by the rules we learned on other stages, e.g., playing child, as well as by rules from stages we have just left or are about to enter. Any single organizational participant, in reality then, is an actor on numerous different stages throughout the day. And the behavior specified as "good" on one stage, e.g., "Con the tourist," may be directly contradictory with those on another, e.g., "Love thy brother." We'll return to this point later, but now let's go back to our motel room.

We still haven't located a place to eat. Remember our organizational "roll book"? Let's review the Yellow Pages. Here we find symbols that participants have constructed to communicate images. Note the specialization in domains. That is, expectations are communicated to us about the central task. However, even though food is served in all of these behavior settings, look at the variety.

But the images conveyed are richer. They contain more than just information about the type of food. Note how the price range is suggested. Restaurants, like any other type of organization vary in prestige as well as task. However, to a degree this aspect of domain is related to the specific task. It would be difficult to create an image of "eliteness" if only hot dogs and soda pop were served. But there is more to it. How are we informed of the prestige ranking? Look again at the Yellow Pages and note the image that emerges as you study a set of symbols that emphasize thrift, speed of service, and standardization of product, e.g., "Our fried chicken tastes the same coast to coast." And the opposite extreme? How is that communicated? Ever see these? "Call for reservations." "Diner's Club, and American Express accepted." Another commonly used device is the title or name; note the use of "prestige by association" through adapted European names. Thus, before we ever reach the location of such a behavior setting, we often have a partial image of what we will find. Indeed, depending on what we want at the time, the image creating symbols guide our selection of one restaurant over another.

Having made a choice and now arriving, let's go inside. We immediately observe the division of labor. All of the participants don't rush over to greet us. In fact, we are pretty much ignored as most continue eating. Others transport trays of food, and a few are cleaning up tables from which previous customers have departed. Recall our earlier comment about uniforms? Task assignment is reflected in varied customs. Upon being seated, we scan the menu and note other cues that reinforce the earlier image. Think for a moment of the variations in food labels and menu designs you have seen.

From our table we can observe the "front stage" and the division of labor found here as part of the organizational task process is completed. This process is comprised of a sequence of behaviors that constitute a not too complex pattern that is repeated over and over again. Thus, customers are greeted by one participant; asked if they have reservations by a second; assigned to a table by a third; and often taken to their table by the second. Water may be poured by a fourth and menus are brought by a fifth. Cocktail orders are taken by a sixth and dinner orders are taken by the fifth after a seventh actor has arrived with some tidbits. Wine with dinner? Sounds great, but don't try to order it from actor five. Of course, he'll be glad to ask number six to return. Afterwards we may be given a bill on a plate on which we are expected to place money or a credit card. And having enjoyed a good meal we are ready to depart.

But this was only the front stage. We don't have a complete description of the task process yet, and we can't until we go "back stage." Of course, dressed for our part as customer, the boundary could be difficult to penetrate. By watching the pattern of movement, we quickly could discover the entrance into one part of it. However, gaining access to the kitchen would most likely require permission. But from whom? Thus, in addition to the kitchen, we would discover another back stage location called the "manager's office." From here, personnel may be assigned, food purchased, and unusual problems—be they customers or health inspectors—are "handled."

This then is an organization as we have and will use the term. It is a patterned interaction system of a special kind. While organizations vary greatly in type of task, degree to which rules are formalized and explicated, and kind of technology used, to mention only a few variables, they are different from nuclear families and communities. How? Clearly they are more complex than the first, and less so than the second. Similarly, for an interaction system to qualify as an organization it must persist over time. A collection of persons who organize for a specific political action drive two weeks before an election which then quickly dissipates, appears to operate differently than a collectivity with greater permanence. If the collectivity continues to assemble after the election, it may *emerge* into an organization. But many short lived social organizations don't, and are not so intended. Organizations then, are *relatively permanent and relatively complex interaction systems.*

EXPLAINING BEHAVIOR PATTERNS[1]

We can observe participant behavior in any organization and describe the behavior patterns just as we did in a very simplified manner in our restaurant example. Of course, we might choose to focus on the communication or decision-making process in addition to the task process or in lieu of it. Depending upon our research interests, our focus might vary in content and detail. There is another type of question, however. That is, why do these patterns persist? And when they change, why do they change and in the direction that they do? Three general and rather abstract concepts can help us a great deal in answering these questions.

First, we would seek to identify the *normative structure.* That is, what are the specific expectations that are guiding the participants? What ranges of behavior are defined as appropriate for persons within this behavior setting? Identification of the normative structure means that we articulate and make explicit the various norms that actors are using. *Norms* are *expecta-*

tions that define a range of tolerable behavior for a given social category of persons. Think back to our restaurant example. The expectations for waiters were not the same for customers or cooks. The script varies depending upon the specific part. But the situation is even more complex. Waiters don't interact with cooks in the same way that they do with customers. Thus, norms are designated as being applicable in some instances and not others. There is structure and pattern; the norms are ordered and clustered.

While there remains disagreement among sociologists as to how various terms ought to be conceptualized, most define the concept of norm pretty much as we have here. Beyond this, however, there is less consensus. You should be aware that some writers in the field define the remaining concepts in this chapter somewhat differently.

In the past few years, greater agreement has been reached on the ones we will discuss. *Clusters of norms which pertain to a given unit of social interaction* are called a *role.* Examples: customer-waiter role; manager-waiter role; cook-waiter role, and so on. Thus, as we penetrate an organization, we seek to ascertain the network of roles and the norms that define the appropriate behaviors of each. *The total collection of roles that are commonly thought to go together* comprise a *social position.* For example, in Figure 3.1 we have diagrammed the social position of the waiter. See the various roles that constitute this social position? If we want to enact the position of waiter and play the part correctly, then we

1. For a more elaborate and detailed development of these ideas see our earlier work: J. Eugene Haas and Thomas E. Drabek, *Complex Organizations: A Sociological Perspective* (New York: The Macmillan Company, 1973), pp. 95–300.

have to know the norms that specify how we are to interact with a whole series of other actors. Review Figure 3.1 and note how these three concepts of norm, role, and social position are interrelated. We could illustrate the same idea by diagramming other networks of role relationships. Try to draw a diagram like that presented in Figure 3.1 for these positions: doctor in a hospital and a public high school teacher.

The specific content of the norms that designate how nurses are to interact with doctors differs from those which prescribe appropriate interaction between busboys and waiters. Think of the variety of norms found within any single organization. Now think of the number of organizations within any single metropolitan area. Imagine the variation. Yet, a nurse may shift from one hospital to another and find that the variation is not all that great. Even if she went to another city, much of what had been learned would still apply. Of course, in every organization we find slight variations, even for specialized occupational categories like "nurse." But then this category, like most others, has many sub-types. There are many types of nurses. Upon trying to identify the

Illustrative Norm: No requests for alcoholic beverages are to be accepted, before, during, or after meals. Refer all requests to cocktail waitress.

Social Position: Network of roles that comprise the position of waiter.

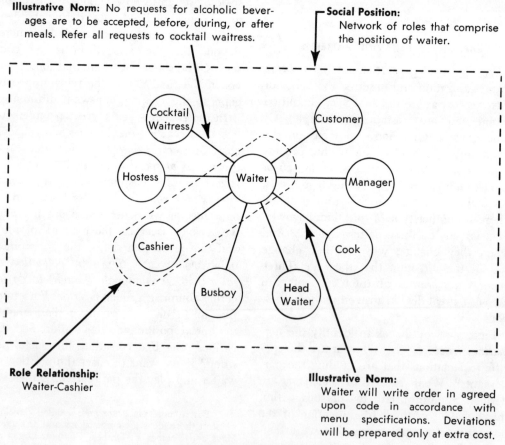

Role Relationship: Waiter-Cashier

Illustrative Norm: Waiter will write order in agreed upon code in accordance with menu specifications. Deviations will be prepared only at extra cost.

Figure 3.1. Being a Waiter

norms that comprise the social position of nurse, we would quickly learn that some norms are applicable to all types while many pertain only to specific ones.

There are certain common features among all social positions if we shift abstraction levels. For example, all are comprised of role relations, even though some are less complex than others. That is, the number of role relationships varies from social position to position. Customers interact with actors who represent only a small portion of the variety found within a restaurant. The social position of manager is more complex than that of a waiter.

There are many other commonalities among role relationships and the social positions they constitute. For example, in all of them we would discover some norms which define the authority dimension. Nurses take orders from doctors, regardless of the individuals acting in each part. Similarly, like head nurses in relationship to nurses, head waiters have a degree of authority over other waiters. In all role relationships, we find some norms that specify who is to have power over whom. However, such authority is limited and carefully defined. There are a few instances like a husband-wife relationship in an egalitarian marriage where neither may have authority over the other and decisions are to be arrived at through mutual consensus, and compromised when necessary. But this is also specified by norms. Just like a waiter who doesn't understand the norms that grant authority to the head waiter, some couples may find their relationship in jeopardy if each spouse has a different definition of the norms. In many organizations authority norms are written down and made formal to reduce such misunderstandings. Often this is done through an organizational chart wherein the various levels of authority are specified and jurisdictional areas are shown.

Norms specify various tasks for each participant in the role relationship. Cashiers do not do the same tasks as busboys. Nor do they engage in the same activities as cooks or managers. A division of labor is created and maintained by norms which specify tasks. When hired as a cook, individuals know they will not be asked to work at the cash register.

Finally, we find norms that specify status in all role relationships. Some social positions have more prestige than others. How would you rank the position of manager versus that of busboy? Norms specify how these status differences are to be evidenced. In large restaurants, many managers will address busboys by their first names. Rarely will we find the reverse. Clothing often reflects status variations, but the variety is infinite. Think of how actors seek to communicate their status rank to us, e.g., formal titles of address (Dr. Smith and Rev. Jones), size of offices, whether offices are private or shared, cost of furnishings (scratched-up metal desk vs. polished walnut) and so on.

In brief, the content of the norms varies from organization to organization and from social position to social position. However, in all role relationships there are norms that specify task assignment, authority, and status differences.

Try to think of other general categories of norms that might be found in all or most role relationships. For example, there are norms specifying affect, i.e., how persons acting in one position are supposed to feel toward persons acting in another. Feelings by persons acting in a husband-wife role relationship are not supposed to be the same as persons acting in a waiter-cook relationship.

Another general category of norms we call *sanctions*, i.e., *norms which specify appropriate behaviors when there is rule violation.* A cook caught spitting into the soup might be fired, but shooting him would not be condoned.

Before leaving the normative structure, we need to add one other concept—*domain.* We have illustrated this term several times earlier, and would define it as *those expectations pertaining to an entire system or subsystem of actors.* Thus, within a large restaurant, there might be a group of four or five persons who comprise a purchasing and food planning unit. Individuals assigned to the personnel office would have very different tasks. At the subsystem level, divisions, departments, directorates, or what have you, reflect another level or layer of norms. Norms for such units, just like those for social positions, are ordered and reflect task, authority, and status differences. The domain of the janitorial unit within a university does not have the same level of status as the physics department or the vice-president's office.

To push one step further, we used this concept domain also to refer to the norms applicable to a total organization. As we illustrated through our discussion of selecting a restaurant, and in the previous chapters, there is a task dimension; we don't try to cash a check at a library. Why? The norms which comprise the domain of banks are not the same as those for libraries. As we saw throughout Chapter 2, there are authority norms that specify the limits of autonomy for various organizations. Just like doctors have the right (and recall Weber's concept of authority, i.e., legitimate power) to direct the activities of cer-

tain nurses, so too local courts have the right to tell school superintendents that the length of a boy's hair is not something they can dictate.

Finally, an important dimension of the domain of any organization has to do with status. Recall our earlier inspection of the Yellow Pages in locating a restaurant? Participants had sought to create a set of images for us. The images varied regarding task, that is, type of food, but also regarding status. Think of the tactics that organization representatives use to try and manipulate the images of their organizations. What they are doing in effect is trying to get us to accept a certain definition of doman.

Thus, there is a dynamic quality to all aspects of the normative structure. At all levels, from the dyad, i.e., a two-person group, which reflects the role relationship level, to a social position, subsystem domain, and system domain, we can envision sets of rules. Such networks of expectations guide the behavior of persons within organizations. But as they interact and are constrained by such expectations, some of their efforts may be directed toward trying to change the rules through renegotiations. The normative structure is never static, it is in a constant state of flux and renegotiation. But human actors are not just rule followers, rather they are more active and they use the rules to guide their behavior. At times, some are very active and seek to use the rules as best they can to further their own interests.

As persons penetrate these structures of rules, they interact with other humans, sometimes over a long period of time. And as they become acquainted, they come to know one another, to varying degrees of course, as individuals. Thus, superimposed over the normative structure is another set of guidelines that we will label the *interpersonal structure*. This term refers to those *expectations which are person-specific*. By June, the students in an elementary school classroom are no longer treated en masse. Bob is different from Dick just as is Sally. Teacher-student interaction is not a product of just the general normative structure which specified what teachers and students are to do. A new order of understandings has emerged that reflect variations among the relationships perceived by the actors involved. There may be a strong feeling of trust and positive sentiment between a teacher and some students. They like one another and may even know quite a bit about each other apart from their organizational performances.

This concept is extremely important. Sometimes you will find a similar concept incorporated into what some writers have called "the informal structure." But as it has been used, this term often includes several other types of ideas such as personality variation. We refer only to interpersonal relationships among two or more actors. These emergent expectations are person-specific, rather than being related to the normative structure. That is, they are expectations that have emerged among specific individuals rather than stemming from the parts or social positions in which each is acting.

Both structures simultaneously guide behavior. But they are not necessarily consistent. The norms may require that all waiters bring checks to the cashier. However, Bill and Don may have an interpersonal relationship which is marked by hostility and distrust. Thus, while Bill (waiter) will still bring checks to Don (cashier), they will interact minimally. We would anticipate that they would look for shortcuts that would reduce their interaction. For exam-

ple, Bill might just leave the check on the cash register desk and then pass by later to pick up the change, or charge slip. Through such tactics, they rarely need to speak to one another. In this way they cope with this strain that is created because the normative structure requires their interaction, but the interpersonal structure precludes it.

Our third concept, the resource structure, is also very broad. Interaction does not take place in a vacuum. The behavior pattern which emerges is affected by the physical setting in which it occurs. Walls, counters, availability of inter-office voice communication, and the like, can and do severely alter interaction. Thus, to understand why a particular behavior pattern persists, we also need to know about the *resource structure*, i.e., *all physical resources used by participants, their ecological placement, and relevant skills of participants*.

To illustrate the importance of this concept, picture a university department comprised of a secretary, chairman, two student assistants, and four professors. They are located temporarily on one floor of a former apartment house. Upon entering the departmental office, you confront the secretary. The student assistants are working at desks located in the same room. Gaining permission from the secretary, we may walk back into the chairman's office or into one of the two offices shared by the professors (see Figure 3.2, TIME ONE). If we observed these persons over a prolonged period of time, interaction patterns among them could be described in detail.

Now assume that one aspect of the resource structure was changed through relocation of their offices into a new building. Note the ecological placement of the offices as depicted in Figure 3.2, TIME TWO. How will the interaction patterns be

TIME ONE

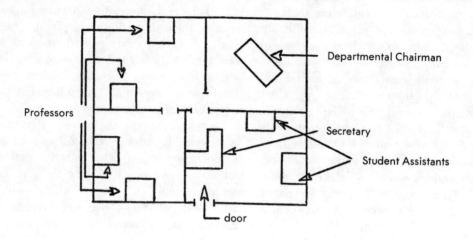

TIME TWO

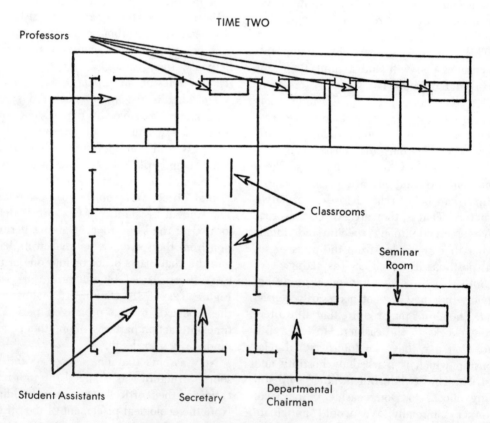

Figure 3.2. Altered Office Locations

changed? Certainly several types of changes could be anticipated despite the fact that the normative and interpersonal structures remained unaltered. Frequency of contact among all of the participants would decrease. And new norms might be expected to emerge since the secretary would never know when the professors were in their offices. As telephone calls or students arrived, she might encounter difficulty in locating them since they might be in a colleague's office, in a classroom, or simply "rapping" out in the hallway. Thus, the resource structure constrains interaction in many subtle but intense ways.

Think of these three networks of concepts, the normative, interpersonal, and resource structures, as placed on top of one another. Perhaps three plastic overlays of differing colors are a good analogy. Individuals are constrained in their behavior by all three simultaneously. As they penetrate the boundary of an organization the first question is one of identity. What part will they play? Are they to be customer, waiter, or manager? Once that is established, they proceed to try and enact the part in accordance with the norms that specify how they are to behave with various other actors. Their interaction is further constrained by the understandings that may have evolved among other actors which are person-specific, i.e., the interpersonal structure. Some they trust and with others they are more guarded. Finally, all of their interaction takes place within a physical setting and is further affected by various types of resources. The doors which enclose the kitchen not only protect this back stage area from the eyes of customers, but also prevent other participants from being in constant view. Taken together, these three structures provide us with a way to understand why a given set

of behavior patterns persist. And note, the behavior specified as appropriate by these three structures need not be consistent. For example, aspects of the interpersonal structure may, and frequently do, conflict with the normative structure.

One part of the normative structure deserves more elaboration because thus far we have referred only to *official norms*. That is *those which are authorized and enforced by various actors in positions of authority*. As anyone who has ever lived in an organization knows, there is another layer of norms. For example, despite the best efforts of a restaurant manager, waiters do get together and as a group may establish their own rules about how things ought to be run. This is not unique to waiters, but has been documented repeatedly in varied kinds of organizations, be they industrial plants, schools, administrative offices, prisons, or hospitals.[2] Let's explore some typical examples to see an additional source of potential conflict.

FREEBIES AND OTHER TYPES OF INDULGENCES

Unofficial norms are found in every organization. That is, *norms which are not officially recognized or enforced by persons occupying positions at a given level in the organization*. Thus, assembly line workers may establish various norms which are not officially sanctioned by their foremen or others above him. Students may establish norms which their teachers cannot endorse, and so it goes. These norms provide power-

2. For example see, Gresham M. Sykes, "The Corruption of Authority and Rehabilitation," *Social Forces*, XXXIV (March, 1956), 257-62; Fritz J. Roethlisberger and William J. Dickson, *Management and the Worker* (Cambridge, Mass.: Harvard University Press, 1939).

ful constraints on behavior, however, despite the lack of official backing.

Probably in every organization we would find examples of freebies which often reflect unofficial norms. Freebies are goods or services which participants define as side benefits of their occupation. Some are official and out in the open like expense accounts. But even these, and many other types as well, may become more "shadowy" and not officially condoned. For example, in all large retail stores some merchandise will get damaged. Or perhaps a toy will be returned because it didn't function properly. Firms vary in their official policies, but in some there emerge unofficial norms which specify what is to be done with such items. What happens to a pair of slacks with a broken zipper, or a shirt with a bad flaw? Some may be given to deserving employees as "freebies." If not free, they may be discounted greatly depending on the degree of damage and the cost of the item. And it is not unheard of for an employee to intentionally create the flaw; like in a shirt tail where it can remain unnoticed when worn.

Once the precedent is established, new supervisors unfamiliar with the norm may receive a variety of signals indicating to them that they are in violation. Much of this communication will be indirect, since workers know that these unofficial norms cannot be approved openly. However, they may suggest them through many strategies. At times they may suggest to a new supervisor that he ought to "look the other way" or simply not be present at a particular time. If he is not there, he can't observe the behavior. Much homosexual activity within prisons is maintained in precisely this way through unofficial norms among inmates.[3]

Freebies come in varying sizes and types. We once heard of a young man who decided to become a fireman. When asked why, he replied that no other job offered him the amount of time that this one did to work on his cars. Of course, if confronted with an incentive to spend time between fires in training programs, we might expect persons like this to remain uninterested. Indeed, he might even react with hostility toward the suggestion. "Imagine, these guys wanting to take away my time." Think about organizations that you know; what varieties of freebies exist there?

This aspect of organizational life is not to be taken lightly as Alvin Gouldner's case study of a gypsum company has shown.[4] Unofficial norms, including those specifying freebies, were carefully documented by him.[5] For example, among the men at this plant, there had emerged a norm that no one should be fired unless they first were given a second chance. As openings occurred elsewhere in the plant, they expected that they would be allowed to bid for them. This was less a means of upward social mobility as it was a way to avoid an unpleasant foreman. Recall the interpersonal structure? This unofficial norm acted as a mechanism to adapt personnel assignments so that strains between the official normative structure and the interpersonal structure could be reduced.

Similarly, if they needed some of the company's tools for work they were doing at home, unofficial norms permitted them to borrow whatever they needed. How's that for a freebie? And there were several others,

3. Rose Giallombardo, *Society of Women: A Study of Women's Prison* (New York: John Wiley and Sons, Inc., 1966).

4. Alvin W. Gouldner, *Wildcat Strike* (New York: Harper and Row, 1965; initially published by the Antioch Press, 1954).

5. *Ibid.*, pp. 18-26.

like understandings defining "protection," i.e., arranging for less strenuous jobs for men injured.

Then a new plant manager arrived who tried to do everything "by the book,"—that is the "book" of official norms. In no time at all, conflicts intensified and shortly thereafter, a wildcat strike erupted. Why were they on strike? The answers were not clear. Violations of unofficial norms are not easy to discuss even though they often arouse intense feelings. So the workers, assisted by their union leaders, sought a grievance that they could discuss openly, like wages. "I mean what else could these men be interested in?" And the real issues never got on the table.

Unofficial norms do not necessarily conflict with official ones. In fact, were it not for the under layer of unofficial norms, much of the work in most organizations simply could not get done. We saw a clear example of this in a police department we were studying a few years ago. Official norms precluded officers answering telephones from talking to the radio dispatcher. But often such conversation permitted more efficiency. In many emergency situations it was absolutely necessary. In unveiling the normative structure of any organization, we must grasp both the official as well as the unofficial components.

ORGANIZATIONS AS ARENAS OF CONFLICT

Too often we hear the idea that persons in organizations are rule-following robots. Undoubtedly some are. But our impression is that many, if not most, are far more active creatures, who seek to use organizational rules rather than be slaves to them. Of course, organizational rule structures vary a great deal in their degree of "tightness."

Much variation is found at differing levels. Generally, the higher up the authority structure one goes, the wider the range of actions permitted. Organizations comprised largely of highly trained persons, like law firms or hospitals, also tend to have looser rule structures than those wherein most are unskilled. Similarly, if the participants are using a technological process which requires that certain actions be taken at a particular instant in time, then we would expect to find rule structures that permit less improvisation. However, too many of our students have displayed an overly rigid imagery. Participants are viewed as entering the behavior setting and moving through it like water running through a complex network of steel pipes. While this imagery may prove useful in analyzing some organizations, we have found that it doesn't fit many. Rather, the constraints are looser and often internally inconsistent. There is room for movement and sometimes considerable room.

This is not to say that organizations are chaos. Patterns in behavior are there. But the constraint structures that most actors confront are not neatly spelled out. There are areas of ambiguity and inconsistency. They are shifting. And they are used. Certain aspects of the normative structure are emphasized more by some than by others. Thus, rather than view this patterned behavior as emerging from a collection of persons who share a common clear cut image of what ought to get done, we suggest a more dynamic approach wherein we view participants as trying to renegotiate existing rule structures to increase their own autonomy, security, and prestige. Cooperation is necessary, but only to a degree. As one moves above the first level in the authority structure, this looser image of organizational constraints appears appropriate. Much behavior is directed at bargaining as actors within each subsystem seek to expand or maintain existing levels of group autonomy.[6] Organizations are made of such struggles and conflicts. See the wide applicability of the concern for autonomy reflected in the "Disk of Oleans"?

But how are these to be understood? Are they simply the outgrowths of personality conflicts or idiosyncratic whims? Let's dig deeper.

We are proposing that both conformity and deviance are found within organizations. Thus far, we have emphasized heavily the conformity aspect where actors play parts according to the rules. But there is deviance as well. Too often the deviance that occurs is viewed simply as a failure by an individual. Given American culture and the values that are emphasized, it is almost impossible for any other view to be considered seriously by most. This is not to deny that some individuals do fail. But when? Why? Why are failure rates higher in some organizations than in others?

In contrast to our argument using the metaphor of the theater stage, let's now emphasize that our participants are actors of a special type. Some, on occasion, simply "play" their parts. They are detached, uncommitted, and uncaring. Most, we suspect, are less alienated. For many, a great sense of self-worth and self-esteem is derived from evaluations made by others of their organizational performance. For these individuals, their participation is not taken lightly. Some are highly intense, perhaps too much so for their own well being. Each person must look at himself. Thus, two critical insights emerge.

First, much behavior that may appear as unpatterned, maybe even deviant, becomes highly meaningful if we shift our imagery.

In addition to viewing persons as being constrained by the normative (both official and unofficial), interpersonal, and resource structures, we need to recognize that there is much bargaining going on. Efforts are being continually made at renegotiation. Persons within subgroups throughout all organizations seek to alter existing constraints. An understanding of the bargaining strategies used is essential if we want to understand these rich and complex behavior patterns. In these bargaining processes, we suspect that participants do not seek only to maximize their own salaries, although that certainly is done. However, for many, increased autonomy, security, and prestige levels for their subdivision is equally important. There is keen competition for such commodities among the department heads of any university, just as there is among the many principals who supervise the schools in your hometown. While they are constrained by many official policies, there remains much room for maneuverability.

But our second point is equally important. Persons within organizations confront structures which are inconsistent. *Structural inconsistencies among various organizational components* will be called *organizational strain*. And it appears that in those systems where the intensity of strain is greatest, we find the highest rates of behaviors that are *labeled* deviant. Let's pursue this idea in more detail.

CONSEQUENCES OF STRAIN

Several years ago, J. Eugene Haas and a group of colleagues analyzed the norms that

6. See Michel Crozier, *The Bureaucratic Phenomenon* (Chicago: University of Chicago Press, 1964), pp. 156-63 and David Silverman, *The Theory of Organizations* (New York: Basic Books, Inc., Publishers, 1971).

comprised the role conception among doctors and nurses.[7] They proceeded to construct a role relations inventory by which they could ascertain the degree of agreement on the norms by various persons who played these parts daily. What did they find? Normative consensus was far more important in predicting the frequency of friction events (arguments) than any other variable. That is, to what degree did the individuals who acted in a specific doctor-nurse role agree on the norms that specified the duties, rights, and responsibilities of the other. Norm dissensus or disagreement represents one type of strain. This study and several others have shown that the more intense the dissensus, the greater the frequency of arguments, friction, and hostility.

Sometimes the strain is of a different order. Teachers receive signals from parents and their professional colleagues that academic excellence is of utmost importance. Yet there is a tightly bound student subculture in many high schools that defines things very differently. Popularity and status do not result from conformity to the norms subscribed to by teachers. Why do teachers cry at times? In part, because they, like many students, confront an organizational structure that contains several types of strain. Not only is there disagreement among them and their principals at times about the norms which should guide their behavior (norm dissensus), but also they often confront sharp inconsistencies in norms.

However, strain is not unique to professionals working in highly bureaucratic structures. Indeed, one national survey found that about half of the workers queried confronted these types of strains.[8] For persons in some types of organizations, e.g., police,

the proportions and intensities may be more severe.[9]

After reflecting on his data collected at the gypsum plant we discussed previously, Gouldner concluded that analysis of such strains—or tensions, as he labeled them—could assist us in understanding not only this particular wildcat strike, but also many other types of organizational changes, be they sudden or more gradual. Think about college campuses you have read about that have experienced mass disruption which is not unlike this wildcat strike in a sense. Our analysis would suggest that charismatic leaders, while necessary, are not sufficient to cause such events. Indeed, at any given time there may be a sufficient richness of personnel on most campuses that finding such leaders always is possible. The critical set of variables appears to be the strains and tensions that participants are confronting and the personal feelings of frustration and even rage that necessarily result when a person does one thing that is expected by one group of actors and receives a reprimand, insult, or some other type of negative sanction from another group. And note one further implication: Attacking the charismatic leaders, or even trying to appease them by making some of the changes they deem important, will not get to the root of the problem. This is merely the very top of the iceberg. Even highly articulate orators

7. J. Eugene Haas, *Role Conception and Group Consensus* (Columbus, Ohio: Bureau of Business Research, Ohio State University, 1964).

8. Robert Kahn, *et al.*, *Organizational Stress: Studies in Role Conflict and Ambiguity* (New York: John Wiley and Sons, Inc., 1964), pp. 55-56.

9. A study of state police found that 90 percent of the officers reported such strains. Jack J. Preiss and Howard Ehrlich, *An Examination of Role Theory: The Case of the State Police* (Lincoln, Nebraska: University of Nebraska Press, 1966).

may lack any insight at all into the network of strains that create expectation structures wherein participants necessarily experience failure. As we gain a better understanding of how to locate such strains and develop mechanisms for reordering them, we can design organizations that are more humane and, in the long run, far more effective.

SUMMING UP

We've come a long way from our motel room where we were reviewing the Yellow Pages in search of a restaurant. We have introduced many themes, some of which we hope you will dig into more deeply. However, there are a few which we view as essential. First, human behavior can be viewed in a collective fashion, wherein we identify behavior patterns, some of which persist over long periods of time. Those that are relatively complex, we call organizations. Human beings participate in these behavior patterns, but they are viewed as active creatures with private thoughts, ambitions, and purposes. We can subdivide the observed behavior patterns into many more specific processes such as task, communication, or decision making.

Why do these behavior patterns persist? Why does the behavior of individuals who are free to come and go as they wish assume such patterning? The answer we propose is that individuals learn norms. However, all norms or expectations are not learned by everyone. Rather we learn about a few specific role relationships, social positions, and subsystem and system domains. As we learn these norms and proceed to behave as we think others expect us to, we receive positive and negative sanctions. That is, in accordance with sanctioning norms, we are treated in a variety of ways. Depending upon the specific social position we are acting in, our degree of freedom is more or less constrained. Normative structures within and among organizations vary greatly; some permit far more freedom than others.

In addition to varying layers of official norms that comprise roles, positions, subsystem domains, and system domains, individuals are further constrained by networks of unofficial norms. Frequently, they may receive negative sanctions from persons around them who resent their violations of these norms. They are further guided by two additional structures of a different order: Interpersonal understandings that have emerged among them and other specific individuals, and the variety and placement of resources controlled by participants. While constrained by these structures, participants remain more or less free within them.

All of these structures should be viewed as dynamic and shifting rather than static. This is because participants, both within and outside the organization, are continually involved in renegotiation of them. Rather than being blind rule followers, most seek to redefine the rules so as to expand the existing levels of autonomy, security, and prestige that are recognized as legitimate for their particular social position, subsystem, or total organization. At times this generates intense competition, but often cooperation is there too, as temporary coalitions are formed to gain the strength necessary to have the renegotiated rule structure accepted.

Behavior patterns persist because of these three structures, each of which is a complex network of substructures. But there are inconsistencies throughout each of the three and among them as well. Confronted with such strained, shifting, and incomplete structures, persons seek to make it through the day. Some days are good, others less so. But a few have learned how to stand back and look at what is going on around them, and ponder why, and thereby take the first step toward a new sense of freedom which can come only through such understanding.

For Further Reading

Barker, Robert G. and Gump, Paul V. *Big School, Small School: High School and Student Behavior.* Stanford, Calif.: Stanford University Press, 1964.

This detailed and systematic analysis of the behavior settings in which high school age students participate and how these settings appear to them as "insiders," revealed that larger organizations, while offering more variation in types of behavior settings, resulted in reduced levels of participation for actors within them.

Blau, Peter M. "Co-operation and Competition in a Bureaucracy." *American Journal of Sociology* LIX (May, 1954): 530-35.

Upon analyzing interviewers in a public employment agency, Blau concluded that friendlier relationships found in one group curbed competition among the participants but gave rise to higher overall group productivity.

Breed, Warren. "Social Control in the Newsroom: A Functional Analysis." *Social Forces* XXXIII (May, 1955): 326-35.

Conflicts among official policy norms set by newspaper publishers and the unofficial norms subscribed to by the staff and the behavior patterns emerging from these tensions are described insightfully.

Gouldner, Alvin. *Wildcat Strike.* New York: Harper and Row, 1965.

After carefully detailing several intense conflicts and changing definitions of them by workers, supervisors, and managers within a gypsum plant, Gouldner shifts abstraction levels and explores a network of analytical propositions through which similar such events and the pattern of tensions which create them can be understood.

Homans, George C. "The Western Electric Researcher." *Human Factors in Management,* rev. ed. Edited by Schuyler Dean Hoslett. New York: Harper and Brothers, 1951, pp. 210-41.

A brief summary of the now classic Hawthorne studies wherein the importance of unofficial norms as regulators of worker productivity were documented through systematic empirical research.

Selznick, Philip. *TVA and the Grass Roots.* Berkeley and Los Angeles: University of California Press, 1949.

Hostile environmental elements were brought into the Tennessee Valley Authority organizational structure, i.e., co-opted, but once there sought to reorder and redirect, as Selznick's case study describes in detail.

Turner, Ralph H. "The Navy Disbursing Officer as a Bureaucrat." *American Sociological Review* XII (June, 1947): 342-48.

Strains among official norms and more informal structures such as friendship patterns are explicated and related to different modal coping patterns used by participants, e.g., regulation types, sincere types, realist types.

Whyte, William F. "The Social Structure of the Restaurant." *American Journal of Sociology* LIV (January, 1949): 302-10.

This rich description of the task process found in restaurants, the normative structure through which it is maintained, and the pattern of strains participants confront, remains one of the best written analyses to date.

4 | Varieties of Organizations

IMAGINE that we are able to observe for one week all of the patterns of interaction that take place within the walls of a public school, a fruit and vegetable canning factory, a state prison, and a local church congregation. Would the patterned behaviors look pretty much alike in all four? And if we were to inquire what was behind the observable patterning, is it likely that we would find that all of these organizations were equally bureaucratic?

How much variation is there among all those social systems we call organizations? Here are some of the kinds of organizations that would be part of any comprehensive list: manufacturing plant, state political party, city recreation department, department store, labor union, religious order, military command, insurance company, police department, television station, farmers lobbying association, state mental hospital, and the U. S. Senate. Knowing only a little about such organizations it is clear that the differences among them are enormous. In some, most participants are volunteers who receive no salary while in others, many of the participants are forced to be there, e.g., inmates. In some instances most members take an active part in deciding what the important policies of the organization shall be,

but in others, only one or a few top executives make such decisions. Some organizations are very large and their employees and buildings are dispersed across a number of nations, e.g., International Telephone and Telegraph Company (ITT). Many organizations are strictly local such as the high school from which you graduated.

What are the really significant ways in which organizations differ? In the subsequent sections of this chapter we will discuss what appear to be some of the most important characteristics of organizations. This will help us think about ways of sorting out organizations into meaningful categories or classes.

AUTHORITARIAN ORGANIZATIONS

Most military units, prisons, and concentration camps tend to be very authoritarian. That is fairly obvious but aren't there others also?

When we speak of the authoritarian mode of organizing we are taking one basic criterion into account: What proportion of the organization's participants play a significant part in determining the organizational conditions that are most important to them? In some church congregations, for example, all members are free to discuss and then decide through voting what they want to transpire in the organization. In other church congregations, the members simply don't have such an opportunity; they are part of an authoritarian system where it is understood that all significant decisions are made by the head of the congregation or perhaps even by his superior who may be called a Bishop. But even in such a highly authoritarian organization, some members serving on committees, may be permitted to make a few minor decisions such as selecting the date and theme for certain social events.

But we should make a distinction between authoritarianism and centralization of decision making. Highly centralized decision making within an organization need not necessarily be a good indicator of authoritarianism. The important question to ask is: Did most participants have a voice in the decision to set up the decision-making process in the first place? If a large majority of the members of the organization were in agreement that the decision-making procedures should be overhauled, could they bring about such a change with relative ease?

In some organizations the participants may expressly determine that they want most of the important organizational decisions made by a few top executives; they vote to have a highly centralized decision-making and authority structure. But they may also expressly reserve the right to re-examine that arrangement and perhaps alter it at periodic intervals, say every two years or every five years. In such a case, we would describe the organization as highly centralized but not highly authoritarian. Thus, while all authoritarian organizations have highly centralized decision-making

and authority structures, not all highly centralized organizations are necessarily authoritarian.

Characteristics Frequently Found in Authoritarian Organizations

A highly authoritarian organization is one in which top officials *alone* make both the broad policy decisions and the internal operating rules and procedures. While no single organization may be completely authoritarian, there are many which come very close to operating in that fashion. Here are some of the other characteristics of such organizations:

a) Detailed job specifications, usually written.

   These job descriptions are usually laid out in such detail that it is clear that the exercise of individual judgment and discretion by the member is *not* wanted. The task and authority dimensions of the various roles are given excessive attention. To the extent that the participant can understand, memorize, and carry out his activities in close congruence with the job description, he or she is safe from citicism from superordinates. One can't be criticized or fired for making "poor decisions" when the job specifications don't permit any decision making at all.

b) Punitive approach to error.

   When rules and job specifications are spelled out in detail, it is easier to tell when someone has made an error. The tendency in authoritarian organizations is to operate on the assumption that the best way to reduce error, whether intentional or unintentional, is to punish those who deviate from the rules. The boss in an authoritarian organization is likely to say, "I don't want to hear about excuses, I'm just informing you that you are being docked one day's pay."

c) High certainty in technology.

The authoritarian mode of organizing is more likely to be utilized where the organization's product or service can be produced under conditions of high certainty. Where such things as cars, paper containers, and electrical power are being produced, there is a well developed technology (both machines and human skills) which, if utilized, can turn out a preferred quantity and quality of product with a very high degree of certainty. The technology for producing "top quality liberal arts college graduates," however, is far from being well understood and thus the level of certainty is lower.

d) Low on creative contribution.

It should not be surprising to learn that in organizations where the "ideal" member is one who carefully follows the written rules and the directives of his superiors, new and creative ideas do not abound. While it is possible for an official to order certain employees to "be creative," it seldom happens that way. Freedom to think and even act in unusual ways seems to be a prerequisite for consistent creative contribution and such freedom contradicts the authoritarian authority structure.

e) High predictability under normal conditions.

In a highly authoritarian organization, the members are really very much like parts of a machine. Their actions are mostly programmed in advance for them, and in the few instances where that does not occur, high officials formulate orders and pass them down the chain of command. The outcome is all very predictable so long as the conditions within and outside the organization remain relatively stable. But if some unusual emergency arises, (e.g., top executives are killed in a plane crash, the building and electrical services are damaged by a hurricane), then the level of predictability decreases sharply. Members who have been trained to follow orders and to avoid using personal discretion can't change that orientation overnight.

How would you try to organize the operation of military combat units? Is a high level of predictability under *most* conditions the ideal? What happens then if units get separated, isolated and are forced by conditions to "fend for themselves"?[1]

DEMOCRATIC ORGANIZATIONS

It should be obvious by now that the democratic mode of organizing is the opposite of the authoritarian mode. In a highly democratic organization, all members who desire to do so may participate in determining how all significant organizational decisions will be made. The set of decision-making procedures that the members agree upon might vary from holding quarterly meetings where issues and questions of all sorts may be raised, discussed and voted upon, to an approach which calls for an annual meeting where the elected Board of Directors reports on the policies, objectives, and outcomes followed by the election or reelection of board members for the next

1. Roger W. Little, "Buddy Relations and Combat Performance," in Morris Janowitz (ed.), *The New Military* (New York: Russell Sage Foundation, 1964), pp. 195-219.

year. We would say that the most democratic organization would be one where member influence is potentially very high (i.e., officially permitted) and where in actual practice there are no serious blocks or impediments to such participation.

It should not be assumed automatically that every organization member wants to be in on every decision that might affect every aspect of his involvement in the organization. Some persons seem to prefer a high level of *non*involvement in decision making especially as regards "routine" decisions. Some high school teachers, for example, say that they get tired of spending so much time in committee meetings trying to reach decisions regarding relatively "unimportant" matters. "The principal is hired to make these decisions, so let him do it," is a view that is sometimes voiced.[2]

Characteristics Often Found in Democratic Organizations

Some organizations are more democratic than others. The most extreme form would be an organization where every member, regardless of his or her particular position in the organization, has an equal opportunity to influence such matters as salary scales, working conditions, length of vacation periods, and even what the principle tasks of the organization should be. Very few organizations are quite that democratic.

For those organizations which are relatively democratic in mode of organization, what are some of their other attributes? What are democratic organizations really like?

a) Personal discretion within job specifications.

Not every member in the organization has the freedom to decide "what shall I do today?" but there is a tendency to have member positions less rigidly structured than in authoritarian organizations. The job descriptions in work organizations are likely to be written in general rather than in detailed language. Supervisors are less likely to be constantly checking up on workers to assure conformity to a rigid set of standards.

b) Low to moderate certainty in technology.

The democratic mode of organizing tends to show up with fairly high frequency in those organizations where the central efforts of the organization are not cut and dried, have not been routinized. Perhaps the best example is a research organization where a variety of highly trained specialists work together on the development of new ideas and techniques. There simply is not agreement among the members that any single way of organizing combined with a specific array of types of equipment will insure that inventions will be forthcoming. The certainty of the outcome is only low to moderate.

c) Decision making is time consuming.

Though it could be done in other ways, a typical procedure used to permit members to participate in significant decisions affecting them is through the operation of committees. This process does provide for the exchange of views and on occasion stimulates some really new ideas. It permits a person from one part of the organization to understand better the problems and concerns of members in other departments and therefore may

2. Melvin Seeman, *Social Status and Leadership: The Case of the School Executive*, Monograph #35, Bureau of Educational Research and Service, (Columbus: The Ohio State University, 1960).

contribute to better quality decisions. But it does take a lot of time. An eight member committee meeting for two hours uses the same amount of organizational time as one person working two full days.

d) More relevant response under unusual conditions.

Where persons are accustomed to having some control over their daily work and even over organizational policies they tend to have a broader perspective. They have learned to be more flexible in their ideas and behavior. As a result, if a very unusual situation develops within the organization (e.g., many absences due to illness) or in the organization's environment (e.g., an economic recession or a flood) the members are able to make relatively quick and more relevant responses. Furthermore, a part of this greater flexibility and relevance is apparently due to the greater sense of commitment to the organization which comes with being involved in significant decision making. If I have something to say about what my organization is doing and becoming, then my sense of pride is tied in with the success of my organization.

TOTAL ORGANIZATIONS

In almost every society there are some organizations which have come to be called total institutions. The word "total" refers to the fact that in these organizations a large proportion of the members are completely encapsulated within the system.[3] While it is true that there are some persons in almost every organization who are said to be "married" to the organization because their whole life and most of their working hours are tied up in the organization, nevertheless we will see that for a certain class of persons, usually called inmates, the involvement in the organization is usually total in every sense of that term.

In many organizations there is a common distinction made between those members who are managers and those who are workers. In total organizations the distinction is usually expressed as the staff and the inmates. Sometimes the latter are called patients as in hospitals or even "guests" as in some nursing homes. The principal difference to note between workers and inmates is that the inmates are under the total control of the staff day and night often for months and years at a time.

The justifications commonly given for using this all encompassing control include punishment, restraint, and rehabilitation. The rationale for putting persons in prisons and concentration camps is the belief that those who have done wrong should suffer by being punished. While there are other ways of punishing wrong-doers, western societies have developed less and less stomach for those measures and have adopted incarceration (imprisonment) as the chief mode of punishment. Thus, for example, there are more than 450,000 persons in various prisons in the U.S. on any given day of the year.[4]

Another justification for encapsulating persons in total organizations is to protect them from hurting themselves and others. They need to be restrained it is said. Persons who are mentally disturbed and physically

3. Erving Goffman, *Asylums* (Garden City, N.Y.: Doubleday and Company, Inc., 1961).

4. President's Commission on Law Enforcement and Administration, *Task Force Report: Corrections* (Washington, D.C.: U. S. Government Printing Office, 1967).

aggressive are treated in this manner. There is also the notion that some persons are "habitual criminals" who can't help committing crimes and therefore must be locked up. Such persons are often given a life imprisonment sentence with the specific stipulation that they may never be released on parole.

The most frequent explanation for putting people in total organizations is that they need to be rehabilitated (cured, re-educated, reformed). We use such interesting labels as reform school, correctional institution, and mental hospital. By whatever name, total organizations are notoriously ineffective in rehabilitating those who have been convicted of criminal acts. Mental hospitals have a cure record which is a bit better but some careful studies have shown that mental patients who don't go to hospitals recover in about the same proportions as those who do become hospital patients.[5]

Another rationale may be seen in those near total organizations in which we place persons who must be "cared for." These include the severely mentally handicapped, the seriously ill for whom there is apparently no hope for recovery and the infirm aged. In essence we put these persons into "refrigeration."

There are other organizations such as religious convents and monastaries where religious values are used as the basis for participating in an almost totally enclosed social system.

Now that we have briefly reviewed some of the principal justifications for the existence of total organizations, let's get more specific about their common features.

Characteristics of Total Organizations

What is the nature of the totality that is involved? In the extreme or pure form a total organization has the following features.[6]

a) Around the clock involvement.
   Encapsulated members are watched, supervised, manipulated or controlled in some manner at all times.

b) Isolation from most outside contacts.
   There is a strong emphasis on sealing off the individual from unwanted influences, including disturbing ideas, germs, and possible weapons and/or plans for escape. This usually involves the use of walls or other physical barriers as well as control over visitors, letters, and phone calls.

c) Control or confiscation of personal property.
   In the extreme form the individual is stripped of all personal possessions including clothing.

d) Scheduling of activities.
   The individual does what has been programmed for him. Sleeping, eating, working, exercising, and even meditating are done when and where the staff decides that they should be. There is no large load of day-to-day decisions to be made here by the encapsulated member.

e) Voluntary entrance and involuntary exit.
   For a few near total organizations such as nursing homes, some mental hospitals and convents, a person may volunteer to become an inmate-like member. I may, for example, decide on my own to enter a hospital for drug addicts. Most persons, however, are forced to join a total

5. Benjamin Pasamanick, Frank Scarpitti, and Simon Dinitz, *Schizophrenics in the Community* (New York: Appleton-Century-Crofts, 1967).

6. Ruth Bennett and Lucille Nahemow, "Institutional Totality and Criteria of Social Adjustment in Residences for the Aged," *Journal of Social Issues* vol. 21 (October, 1965): 44-78.

organization. Once a person becomes a member of any total organization, it is the staff or perhaps a court that determines when, if ever, the inmate may leave.

f) Effective sanctions applied.

When you are in a total organization you behave in conformance with the rules and schedules set up for you. Failure to do so may find you in a straight jacket, a solitary confinement cell or hungry after meal time. When you are encapsulated in a total organization you have almost no power to blunt the will of your "captors."

There are some interesting variants from this totality theme. Some organizations try to approximate the control of total organizations without necessarily having the "subjugated" members enclosed by physical walls or barriers. For example, the Old Order Amish, a separatist religious denomination usually live in rural areas. They live on family-owned farms which tend to cluster in certain areas but there are also many non-Amish families living nearby. They have their own schools, wear distinctive clothing and do not own cars, radios or televisions. These and other practices are designed to keep contact high within the Amish and to an absolute minimum with non-Amish persons. Though some young Amish do defect from time to time, the insulation effort is generally effective, and each local congregation or organization has been able to maintain most of its distinctive features through this nearly total lifelong socialization process of its members.[7]

Similarly, Selznick found that some conspiratorial political parties, such as the Communist Party in the U.S.A. during the 1930's, carefully planned to absorb all of the new party member's time and to encourage social contacts only with other party members.[8] Again the apparent intent is to make the influence and control over the member as total as possible without having forceable physical separation.

VOLUNTARY ORGANIZATIONS

"Voluntary Associations" is a standard term in sociological literature. Given what we said in the preceding section, it would be reasonable to conclude that any organization which isn't a total organization must therefore be a voluntary organization. Unfortunately it isn't quite that simple. Membership in some organizations is more voluntary than in others. For example, many persons are "born into" a particular church organization and have just never bothered to specifically affirm or retract that membership tie. But one doesn't just "accidentally" become a member of the Rotary Club or the League of Women Voters in that same way. Similarly there seems to be a difference between being employed full time in an organization for salary or wages, and participating on a part-time basis as a member of a club or association. We wish then to single out those organizations which seem to be the extreme opposite of total organizations. They entail the least comprehensive member involvement of any kind of organization. Most or all of the participants are involved only on a part-time basis. We call them voluntary organizations.

These voluntary organizations cover the range of general interest associations such

7. J. A. Hostetler, *Amish Society* (Baltimore: Johns Hopkins Press, 1963).

8. Philip Selznick, *The Organizational Weapon: A Study of Bolshevik Strategy and Tactics* (New York: McGraw-Hill, 1952).

as the Chamber of Commerce and the Sierra Club which purportedly are concerned with general civic betterment, special stratum interest groups such as war veteran associations and the PTA (Parent-Teachers Association), and what might be called "special-individual interest groups" such as the National Rifle Association and the American Association for the Advancement of Science.

But whatever the domain of the voluntary organizations—broad and vague or narrow and specific—there are some common characteristics which appear to exist rather generally among them. First, participation in these organizations is segmental. For most members, involvement represents only a small fraction of their time, attention, and self image. For example, I might be a member of Common Cause, a citizens lobby organization started by John Gardner in an attempt to give unorganized citizens a chance to influence governmental decisions. I pay my yearly dues, receive a newsletter and other reading materials which I read from time to time, and on occasion I mail in an extra contribution. I am proud to be a member of Common Cause but I seldom have any face-to-face contacts with other members of the organization. Such involvement is indeed far from total. It represents only a very small segment of my life. If I participate in a bowling league or a political party, my participation level will probably be greater but it is still likely to be a relatively limited segment of the total activity in which I engage.

As a voluntary organization becomes larger and larger, a paid staff of employees is hired to assist in the conduct of the business of the organization. They are supposed to carry out the policies and procedures approved by the members of the voluntary organization. At first these employees may be hired on a part-time basis but so long as membership dues or other sources of income for the organization are adequate or expanding it isn't long before many of the employees are paid on a full-time basis. And it is precisely because the staff are full time and regular members are only segmentally involved that the staff often develops a large degree of influence over the policies and principal activities of the organization. It is almost as though the employees have developed into the bosses of the organization.[9]

But if the level of member participation in a voluntary organization is limited, the extent to which the norms of the organization have a restricting or constraining influence on members is limited too. Absenteeism and turnover are persistent problems. Members are not employees in the usual sense and, therefore, can't be fired for being inadequately productive. If the rules are too strict, for example a rule stipulating that any member missing more than two consecutive meetings will lose membership, then total membership may decline thus threatening the survival of the organization or at least one unit of it.

Since member participation isn't based on wage and salary payment, how is it that participation exists at all? How can such organizations exist? There is undoubtedly a multitude of individual reasons why so many persons are involved, however slightly, in so many organizations. It is likely that many persons find membership in voluntary organizations helps them to avoid boredom. In general, though, it seems that the

9. Robert Michels, *Political Parties*, trans. Eden Paul and Cedar Paul (New York: Free Press, 1949; original publication, 1915).

activities of the organization and the symbolic rewards attached to being a member are the variables promoting participation. If I like to bowl or feel especially comfortable in the company of bowlers, I may join the bowling league. If I am skilled at bowling so that at least on occasion I finish at or near the top of the scoring and consequently receive the acclaim of my fellow bowlers along with a trophy or prize money, then I am very likely to join that voluntary organization and continue to be a member for an extended period of time. On the other hand, I may later find that the activities of the Daughters of the American Revolution or the local chapter of the American Red Cross are more to my liking and substitute participation there for that of the bowling league.

This case of substitutability points to another characteristic of voluntary organizations. The ongoing organization does not have a high degree of boundary control. Participants may enter and exit with relative ease quite unlike the typical setting for a total organization. While there are some exceptions, most voluntary organizations do not have highly restrictive entrance requirements. Entrance rites are relatively simple or nonexistent. If what a voluntary organization "has to offer" no longer has high attraction to a member, there won't be any significant restrictions on exiting. There may be some interpersonal ties which tend to bind but there is very little else that would make it difficult to withdraw from participating. There is no exit interview as in some business firms and certainly no such thing as an examination by a medical committee or a parole board to determine the "fitness" of the member for departing the organization. The boundaries of voluntary organizations are analogous to very course sieves, quite unlike the walls and guards which maintain the boundary of a total organization.

Finally, we should note that the nature of most voluntary organizations means that it is more difficult to mobilize them for unusual and sustained action. The notion of command and control by top management is unusual in these organizations. There may be occasions, as with political parties, religious sects and, more recently, environmental organizations, when the ideological beliefs of the members provide a basis for remarkably intense activities such as door-to-door canvassing. But such intense, coordinated efforts seldom last more than a few weeks or months at most.

We turn next to the consideration of an organization-environment dimension which sorts out organizations in yet another way; the extent to which an organization has competitors to deal with. If an organization has no competition in its environment we say that it is a monopolistic organization. If there are many competitors engaging in real competition we say that it is a competing organization. There are, of course, many organizations which fall in between these two extremes. Our aim in this discussion, however, is to point to the contrasts between these two varieties and to indicate some of the associated consequences.

COMPETING ORGANIZATIONS

We usually think of competition existing among business firms and between political parties. We are less likely to note the competition among the various religious organizations (congregations) within a city or between various mens' service clubs such as Rotary, Lions, and Kiwanis. Indeed, even so-called charitable organizations seem to compete over which disease entity or disability shall be within the domain of any given organization. The Tuberculosis Society has attempted in recent years to change its domain and its name to include all respiratory diseases. Many other examples could be given.[10] But that should not be surprising since a tendency which is basic to all organizations is to take actions to maintain or increase the autonomy, security, and prestige of the organization. If there are competitors in the environment who could reduce the autonomy, security, and prestige of an organization, we would fully expect an organization to take action to counter that threat from the competition. Thus, competition does not only involve the sale of products or services.

What are some of the characteristics of organizations which have many competitors, many segments of the environment which can threaten their autonomy, security, and prestige? First, there is evidence of much attention being given to the potential non-survival (security) of the organization. This may be evidenced in a variety of ways such as stress on employee loyalty, efficiency in the work process and added emphasis on protecting "company secrets." The generalized concern with organizational survival is the characteristic to be noted. The particular ways in which that concern is expressed may vary markedly from one organization to the next.

Competing organizations also tend to have well developed, established procedures for monitoring the environment, especially the competing segments of the environment. It is true that there is a sameness about organizations engaged in similar activities. They tend to follow what is considered "good" or "safe" practices regardless of the level of competition each faces. There are traditions and fads in or-

ganizational policies just as there are in clothing styles. Nevertheless, organizations which face a higher level of competition do, on the average, show more consistent efforts to monitor the environment than those with less competition. At least, that appears to be the case.

A third characteristic of competing organizations is their greater tendency to change their principal activities and their internal normative structure (policies, rules, departmentalization, positions). The reasons for such flexibility are not as obvious as one might guess. Undoubtedly a generalized concern for organizational survival and the many bits of information that come from systematic monitoring of the environment may make these organizations more change oriented. But it is also possible that the environmental feedback from monitoring reveals that maintaining the *status quo* is most likely to contribute to increased security. And again there seems to be a general acceptance in certain types of organizations of the slogan, "Either an organization changes or it dies." So the reasons why competing organizations change more than others are complex and at this point they are not well known. Also, we should be aware that some organizational changes are mostly symbolic and superficial. They represent name changes, perhaps even changes in written policies but a careful examination of ongoing organizational activity would reveal only a superficial alteration of the organization's basic activities. We are

10. David Sills, *The Volunteers,* (Glencoe, Ill.: Free Press, 1957); Robert A. Scott, "The Selection of Clients by Social Welfare Agencies: The Case of the Blind," *Social Problems* 14:3 (Winter, 1967): 248-257; John R. Seeley, B. H. Junker, and R. W. Jones, Jr., *Community Chest* (Toronto: University of Toronto Press, 1957).

suggesting that competing organizations give evidence of significant organizational change more often than do others.

Finally, competing organizations engage in more attempts at manipulating the environment.[11] They tend to be activist organizations. Much of the attempted manipulation involves notions of organizational domain. "Our organization is unique. It can provide a range of services and quality of products not available from any of our competitors." Manipulation efforts also include lobbying, political sabotage, and even in contributing both money and time to such civic efforts as the United Way campaign.

There are several relevant trends that should be noted. The last several decades have seen a rapid increase in the number of corporate conglomerates in existence. One way for a business firm to try to cope with competition is to buy controlling interest in smaller competing firms. After absorbing several such firms, the young conglomerate may buy out or merge with some large organizations, some of which may engage in very different types of business. Now the assets of the combined companies are such that the conglomerate can often dominate the competition.

Middle sized and large business firms frequently monitor the environment by hiring someone to conduct market research to try to gain a better understanding of why the product is or isn't being purchased by various types of customers. Sometimes when a new and relatively distinct product or service is being planned, market researchers will attempt to ascertain in advance how acceptable or desirable the product or service is in the view of potential customers. Another monitoring technique entails systematic price comparisons. Where prices may fluctuate with some frequency such as

in supermarkets, it is not unusual to have an employee or hired firm go to the competitor's locations and carefully record prices on key items.

And then there is the Madison Avenue delight—advertising. "You must advertise to stay alive" is the theme. If the competitors don't advertise or do so only a little, then attempting to manipulate the public by advertising may be an effective approach to increasing organizational autonomy, security, and prestige. Most of the time it appears that everybody advertises, so that if my organization invests in advertising there is no particular advantage. I may conclude, and will certainly be told by advertising representatives, that my organization must advertise in self-defense. So everyone spends money on advertising but it is probably fair to say that the only benefactors are newspaper, magazine, billboard, radio, and television companies. Whether much actual manipulating of the intended public occurs as a result of all this ear and eye battering of advertising is a moot point. Nevertheless, the game continues to be played with deadly seriousness in most non-Communist societies.

MONOPOLISTIC ORGANIZATIONS

There are some organizations which are very secure. They have no competitors at least in the sense of overlapping domains. A state prison, public school system, a fire department and an electric utility company are examples of organizations that will continue to exist into the indefinite future. The view that is broadly accepted is that the

11. Charles Perrow, *Complex Organizations: A Critical Essay* (Glenview, Ill.: Scott, Foresman and Company, 1972), see especially pp. 177-204.

service or product which each monopolistic organization provides is so basic and the demand for it so consistent that somehow or other the organization must continue to function. There may, on rare occasions, be externally based attempts to change the organization, as for example, the U.S. Post Office in recent years, but there are almost never any serious efforts at disbanding the organization.

Thus, one of the characteristics of these organizations is the absence of generalized concern over survival. Certainty of survival may not be complete but it is generally understood by the participants to be nearly so. But it should not be assumed that because survival is virtually assured that no efforts are made to monitor the environment or to manipulate segments of that environment. Even these organizations are not immune to considerations of autonomy, security and prestige. It would appear, however, that the monitoring and manipulation efforts are fewer and more specialized. Since most of these organizations receive their principal financial input from public funds and are, in addition, at least nominally under the supervision of other organizations, it should not be surprising to learn that attempts at monitoring and manipulation are focused on those legislative and executive bodies such as Congress, state legislatures, city councils and various regulatory agencies.

Change is infrequent for monopolistic organizations. Some changes, of course, are forced on the organization by a superordinate organization such as a legislature, but internally promulgated change seems to be relatively infrequent. There appears to be a lot of copying when it does occur. An organization will initiate internal change apparently as a result of the fact that some other similar organizations have set the pattern of change. For example, a city public works department will alter its divisional structure after several other "respected" public works departments in other cities have lead the way. Thus, in a real sense, this type of change is reference group oriented.

While it is difficult to document satisfactorily, it appears that monopolistic organizations are not particularly successful in attracting specialized personnel, especially when such personnel are in short supply. This type of competition seems inevitable. Most monopolies, being supervised to some extent by superordinate organizations, appear to have less flexibility to alter job characteristics and accompanying salaries and wages. When there is a significant shift in the job market or when rapidly increasing salaries are escalating along with an inflationary trend, nonpublic organizations may adjust, at frequent intervals, the salaries and fringe benefits being offered new employees while the response time for public monopolistic organizations is much slower.

The client or customer orientation of monopolistic organizations tends to be weak. It is not that all of these organizations treat clients with indifference or hostility nor do all competing organizations have a strong, positive customer orientation, but on the average the customer-client will receive treatment less in keeping with his preferences when he is interacting with a monopolistic organization.

Other examples of monopolistic organizations not mentioned above include military organizations, police, telephone company, court system, distributors of natural gas and in most communities the public library. If you consider the various departments of city, county, state, and the federal government as separate organizations, you will get some idea of the very large number of such organizations which are intertwined in our daily lives.

OTHER TYPOLOGIES OF ORGANIZATIONS

There have been a number of other ideas presented regarding how the great variety among organizations could be simplified by classification. Talcott Parsons, a well known author of social theory, has suggested that organizations can be sorted into classes based on the character of their output or contribution to the functioning of society as a whole. One type of organization, Parsons points out, is the production organization. This type of organization produces goods and services utilized in the society. Production organizations deal with what Parsons calls societal adaptation. Organizations that deal with goal attainment for the society are essentially political or power distributing organizations (e.g., military). The third type is the integrative organization. These organizations participate in resolving conflicts and ensuring that parts of society work together. Included in the final type, according to Parsons, are pattern maintenance organizations which engage in the perpetuation of basic societal value patterns (e.g., schools and churches).[12]

Peter Blau and W. Richard Scott, based on their own extensive organizational research, have outlined a four part classification scheme. They argue that what really separates organizations into meaningful classes is the criterion of *cui bono* or who benefits.[13] Thus, mutual benefit associations are operated in such a way that the members of the organization itself are the prime beneficiaries. Business concerns are the type where the owners gain all or most of the benefit, whereas when service organizations operate as they should, the clients are the prime beneficiaries. Finally, there are commonweal organizations where the prime beneficiary is said to be the public-at-large (e.g., Congress).

Amitai Etzioni's approach is to examine the power relations between top management and what he calls lower participants.[14] Thus, when managers use coercion on the lower participants, it produces alienation, a kind of negative involvement. These are called coercive organizations. Where the power relation is based primarily on remuneration, the involvement of lower participants tends to be calculative or utilitarian and thus we have a type labeled utilitarian organizations. The final type includes organizations where the power relation rests in ideological and normative ideas (e.g., religious order, political party) and the involvement is said to be moral in nature. These are normative organizations.

None of the above typologies have proven very useful so far. It appears that they are too simplistic or, at least, none has successfully noted the really key characteristics which would separate horses from rabbits, as it were.[15]

There is another research trend that suggests the possibility of a useful typology of organizations. Charles Perrow in the United

12. Talcott Parsons, "Suggestions for a Sociological Approach to Theory of Organizations," *Administrative Science Quarterly* 1 (June, 1956): 63-85.

13. Peter M. Blau and W. Richard Scott, *Formal Organizations*, (San Francisco: Chandler Publishing Company, 1962).

14. Amitai Etzioni, *A Comparative Analysis of Complex Organizations*, (New York: Free Press, 1961).

15. Richard H. Hall, J. Eugene Haas, and Norman J. Johnson, "An Examination of the Blau-Scott and Etzioni Typologies," *Administrative Science Quarterly* 12 (June 1967): 118-139.

States and Joan Woodward in Great Britain are probably the two best known proponents of what might be called a technological perspective.[16] It is obvious, of course, that the focus of activity in some organizations is on processing physical objects or materials of some kind, while in others the focus is on doing things to or with persons. So it is argued that organizations are systems which use energy in a patterned, directed effort to alter the condition of basic materials in a predetermined manner. In this context then, technology is defined as the actions that an organizational member performs on an "object," with or without the aid of tools in order to change the object. "Objects," of course, may be physical things, persons or symbols (e.g., developing new ideas from old ones as in inventions). There are two key issues or questions growing out of this broadened definition of technology. How well is the raw material understood? For example, for schools, how well are the learning processes of young children understood? Presumably, in a milk packaging plant, processing the basic material, milk, is a well understood procedure. The second basic question is, how uniform is the material? In a typical first grade class there are likely to be a few brilliant children who already read very well and also a few who are at the opposite extreme. Standard processing techniques may work well on most children in the class, but the bright and the dull ones are the exceptions. The frequency with which such exceptions have to be taken into account is a key to the type of technology that will be used. So, four types of organizations emerge from the cross tabulation of these two dimensions: 1) organizations having a well understood raw material which requires few or no exceptions in technology; 2) organizations with well understood material but requiring adjustment to many exceptions; 3) organizations dealing with materials that are not well understood but the material is relatively uniform; 4) organizations dealing with not very well understood materials which require numerous exceptions to the standard technology being used.

Neither Perrow[17] nor Woodward[18] have claimed that all organizations fall neatly into one type or another, but the basic idea is an intriguing one. Do organizations which have the first type of technology differ in numerous other ways from organizations with the fourth type? The basic idea appears to be worth careful research.

MAKING SENSE OUT OF CHAOS

It should be clear by now that social scientists have not yet developed classification procedures for social phenomena in general, or even for specific social systems called organizations that are at all like the taxonomic schemes used in botany and zoology. Are such sorting or taxonomic approaches really needed?

By now you probably have a sense of the incredible variation among organizations. Each organization we might examine is different from any other in certain respects and similar to all others in some other ways. As we have seen, the array is so great that really useful classification schemes haven't been developed yet. What appears to be

16. J. Eugene Haas and Thomas E. Drabek, *Complex Organizations: A Sociological Perspective* (New York: Macmillan, 1973), pp. 73-83.

17. Charles Perrow, "A Framework for the Comparative Analysis of Organizations," *American Sociological Review* 32 (April, 1967): 194-208.

18. Joan Woodward, *Industrial Organization: Theory and Practice* (London: Oxford University Press, 1965).

needed is some method of sorting organizations into a number of classes or types so that there is a good likelihood that certain fairly specific propositions or generalizations will be found to be valid within at least one of the classes of organizations.

This approach, of course, is the basic perspective of science. The aim is to try to avoid getting caught up in the idiosyncratic details of each case that we examine and instead to focus on those abstract variables which, if properly measured, will help us answer a number of interesting questions about what is going on within one or a few classes. For example, consider the question, why are member turnover rates so much higher in some organizations than in others? If you attempt to research that question on a wide variety of organizations such as churches, schools, factories, prisons, military units, and the U.S. House of Representatives, the chances are that you simply won't be able to find *any* even moderately satisfactory answers to the question. But suppose that we had a well developed taxonomy of organizations (comparable to the notions of phylum, class, order, family, genus and specie used in zoology) then it would be possible to test hypotheses about member turnover, within a single class—say on voluntary organizations that have a strong ideological basis for member involvement. Under such circumstances the likelihood of finding meaningful answers would be greatly enhanced.

The typologies reviewed earlier have an intuitive base. The authors thought that the variables they used ought to be the significant ones to sort out organizations. The taxonomic approach, however, proceeds in a different way. Here the strategy is to locate a large sample of phenomena and then look for critical features to emerge in the process of sorting the many cases in the sample. Consider, for example, how you would have viewed animals prior to the time of Linnaeus. Would it have occurred to you to place a bat, a whale, and a human into a similar taxonomical niche? Hardly! But careful examination of many cases led to the conclusion that these three did have a basic similarity, did belong to the same class in the sense that they did have certain abstract characteristics in common.

Such an *empirically based* taxonomy of organizations is what is needed. Several pioneering efforts have been made[19] but the task will require a great deal more creative work. Here is a place where you might make a really significant contribution to the theory and understanding of organizations.

Now let's consider individual organizations in a broader context. We will examine next the links between organizations and the networks that emerge.

For Further Reading

Abrahamson, Mark. *The Professional in the Organization.* Chicago: Rand McNally, 1967.
  This book provides an opportunity to see the extent to which professionals have similar challenges and problems regardless of the particular kind of complex organization within which they operate. Reports research findings on scientists, physicians, nurses, ministers and even psychologists.

Bell, Gerald D., ed. *Organizations and Human Behavior.* Englewood Cliffs, N.J.: Prentice Hall, 1967.

19. J. Eugene Haas, Richard H. Hall, and Norman J. Johnson, "Toward An Empirically Derived Taxonomy of Organizations," in Raymond V. Bowers (ed.), *Studies on Behavior in Organizations,* (Athens, Georgia: University of Georgia Press, 1966), pp. 157-180 and Derek S. Pugh, David J. Hickson, and C. Robin Hinnings, "An Empirical Taxonomy of Structures of Work Organizations," *Administrative Science Quarterly* 14 (March, 1969): 115-125.

A potpurri of articles which represent a fair cross section of the work published up to that date on organizations and occupations. Includes such intriguing titles as, "The Red Executive," "The Block Buster," and "The Cab Driver and His Fare: Facets of a Fleeting Relationship."

Cressey, Donald R., ed. *The Prison: Studies in Organization and Change.* New York: Holt, Rinehart and Winston, 1961.

If you haven't served time in a prison or as a guard this book will be interesting and informative.

Etzioni, Amitai. *A Comparative Analysis of Complex Organizations.* New York: The Free Press, 1961.

A thoughtful attempt to compare organizations by looking at their internal power relations and the ensuing consequences.

5 | Networks of Organizations

PICK any organization that you know reasonably well. How many relatively distinct groups can you identify within the organization? If it is a work organization, it is likely that the tasks of the various groups are linked together through the application of rules and policies which indicate how the activity or product of one group is supposed to "feed into" or make possible the work of other groups. The groups taken as a whole are linked together in a way that makes it clear that they are a kind of network. There is interdependence among them. It would be hard to imagine one of the groups continuing to operate over a long period of time entirely alone, without any contact with the other groups. It is this interdependence among the units (groups) which makes it reasonable to speak of an organization as a social *system*.

Looking at intra-organization (one part of which is intergroup phenomena) activity and structures comprises one level of organizational analysis. A second level of analysis is one where we analyze what goes on among and between organizations. Any particular organization is always linked with at least some other organizations. Therefore, we can select one organization, take note of the other organizations with

which there is repeated interaction and perhaps interdependence, and view those links as comprising a network. Any organization exists within a network of other organizations. It never stands alone.

THE HOUSE THAT JACK BUILT

To illustrate the network concept, let's examine the range of organizations that are likely to be involved when someone decides to build a house. How many different organizations do you suppose are directly involved with the house that Jack built? Here is a partial list:

1. The lot or "acreage" was purchased from a land investment company through a local real estate organization.
2. The accuracy of the boundary lines was checked by a local surveying firm.
3. As further precaution against any unexpected land claims in the future, the title to the property was insured by a title insurance corporation.
4. Then an architectural firm was engaged to design the house and draw up the technical specifications which were given to—
5. Several general building contractors who prepared bids.

6. One of these companies was awarded the bid as general contractor. But before he submitted his final bid he secured bids from at least two each of the following kinds of subcontractors:

Plumbing   Landscaping
Heating   Plaster
Excavation   Painting
Electric   Floor covering
Roofing

7. But before any work could begin a building permit had to be secured from a local governmental department which could give the permit only after a zoning and planning commission had completed its work for the specific area. Its work in turn had to be approved by the city council or county commissioners.

8. A building permit can be given legally only if, A) a sewer department or a sanitary district agrees to the hook-up or there is an adequate substitute way of disposing of sewage, B) a water department or company will provide water or there is an adequate substitute, C) the electric power company says okay, and D) there is available some type of fuel for heating such as natural gas, propane, fuel oil or coal.

9. Unless Jack has a large number of readily available dollars, he will probably secure a mortgage from a savings and loan association and that loan may be insured by an agency of the Federal government.

10. The general contractor will have an insurance company write a policy to covers his laborers, materials, and general liability.

11. When construction gets underway, the general contractor will secure supplies and equipment from most of the following companies which are in addition to the subcontractors and their suppliers:
lumber yard
window company
rock and gravel quarry
cement
specialty wood products
portable toilets

12. Unless it is a large general contracting firm, various companies will be contacted to provide:
cabinet work
cement finishing
gutters and downspouts
fencing
masonry
window cleaning
ceramic tile work

13. While the house is under construction, it will be checked periodically by building department inspectors to see that all work conforms to the local version of the Uniform Building Code.

14. The contractor and subcontractors will be making payroll tax deductions for all employees and sending the money to the Internal Revenue Service.

15. The general contractor and many of the subcontractors will be members of a contractors association and the workers on the job are likely to belong to several labor union organizations.

16. Finally, when Jack moves into his new home, he will undoubtedly have arranged with his local insurance agency to have a homeowners insurance policy provided by a national insurance company.

Now, what was your guess as to the number of organizations directly involved in the house that Jack built? If you guessed between 50 and 60 you were in the right ballpark. And note that in most cases we did not mention any of the organizations involved in the extracting, transporting, processing, assembling, warehousing, advertising, inventing, patenting, legally regulating, taxing, and distributing of raw materials, products and services prior to their reaching the organizations that were directly involved in Jack's home construction project. To count the organizations involved in those processes also would add perhaps several hundred more organizations to our list. And the furnishings haven't even been secured yet!

But a modern house is a complex physical structure so perhaps the large number of organizations involved isn't too surprising.

Let's take something simple such as the sugar you may put in your cup of coffee at home. What could be less complicated than getting sugar, especially sugar made from sugar beets within the United States. It doesn't involve overseas transportation or foreign currency exchange. Getting sugar on the table is really quite simple, or is it?

Examine Figure 5.1. It represents an outline of the processes and organizations involved in getting that sugar for your coffee to you. It suggests that there are at least 220 different organizations linked together in a kind of loose but necessary network. While a few of the types of organizations could perhaps be removed from the network without promptly stopping the flow of sugar to you, it is fairly clear that each of the estimated 220 organizations is a significant link in the *horizontal* web or network.

We use the term horizontal here to distinguish this relationship between organizations from the hierarchial relation which we will treat in the next section. As Figure 5.1 should suggest to you, the organizations indicated are linked together. There is considerable interdependence involved. And note that it is *inter*dependence. That is, the dependence goes both ways. The sugar producer is clearly dependent on all of the organizations involved in the production of the sugar beets and the transporting of them to his processing plants. But he is also dependent on the wholesaler and his collateral organizations, the retailer with his collateral organizations, and the consumer or perhaps we should say the final purchaser. So there can't be much question about the interdependence among the various organizations in the web.

That same type of interdependent network is repeated literally thousands of times within a modern technological society. Just note a few of the products and services that you use everyday and for each try to make a chart comparable to Figure 5.1.

We refer to the links among organizations in such networks as horizontal links. Note that while there is interdependence there is also a fair measure of autonomy for any given organization. A particular retailer may not want to continue buying from a specific wholesaler. At least in large cities he has the option of purchasing all or part of his products from a different wholesaler. Similarly, while the wholesaler is dependent on some sugar producer he may not be dependent on any specific producer. No sugar producer has authority over a particular grocery wholesaler. They may negotiate about price or delivery dates but neither can force the other very far. Thus, horizontal links are ties between relatively independent organizations where there is repeated interaction but no established authority relation between them. The organizations are spread on the flat surface of a map, so to speak.

73

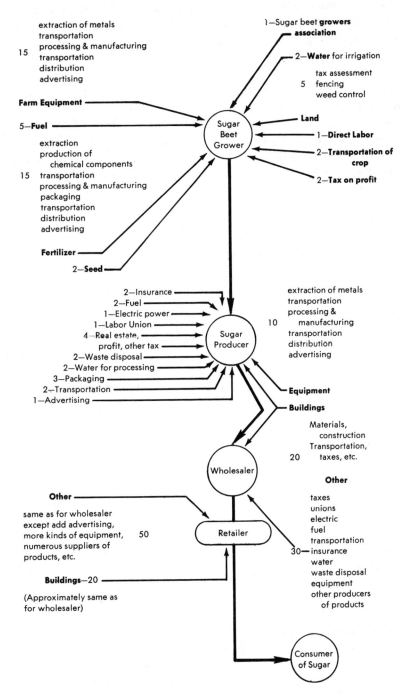

Figure 5.1. Outline of Processes and Number of Organizations Involved in Providing Sugar to Consumer

LAYERS OF ORGANIZATIONS

Now we should change our map analogy to a three-dimensional topographic map. When you put your fingers on the map, you can easily feel where the mountains and valleys are without looking. Organizations are also linked *vertically* into networks.

Take the case of some of the departments of the executive branch of the Federal government in the United States: Health, Education and Welfare (HEW), Housing and Urban Development (HUD), Transportation (DOT), and Labor (DOL). Each department has a national office with a large staff in the Washington, D. C. area. In addition, most such departments have regional offices around the country. Each of these offices has its own quarters and personnel; each is a separate organization in many ways. In recent years there has been an effort to put into effect a policy of decentralization or regionalization. While general broad policies for the department should still be established at the Washington (national) level, the regional organizations should have wide discretion in making substantive decisions on programs, research and development grants, and similar matters. The regional organizations of the different departments within a single region may have repeated direct interaction on matters of very significant import. For example, the Federal Regional Council for Region 8 meets regularly in San Francisco. It is composed of the heads of many of the regional organizations of the federal departments mentioned above. The states in that region are more earthquake prone than any other part of the country so one of the Federal Regional Council's projects is to work together on research and planning in the hope that when the next big earthquake comes, the losses will be smaller and their organizations better prepared to assist in relief and rehabilitation efforts.

You may ask, "Why should we consider the regional office of a federal department of government as a separate organization?" Good question. It brings us back to the definition of an organization. An organization is a complex, discernible interaction system. It is not always obvious where the boundaries of any specific organization are. Some researchers might want to draw the boundaries at different places than would others. Should the entire federal government be considered a single organization? That would include all of the departments, the independent agencies such as the Atomic Energy Commission, the House of Representatives and the Senate as well as the Supreme Court. Indeed, that would include all of the employees of the federal government wherever they might be in the world or in outer space. For certain purposes, it would be reasonable to say that all of the federal government is a single organization. For other purposes, it would be reasonable to view each major component as a separate organization, e.g., Department of Defense, National Aeronautics and Space Administration, U. S. Senate, etc., because each is a clearly discernible, separate social system. It is not just their names that differ. That isn't important. The identifiable activities that they do are clearly different. Each can be distinguished from the others because it engages in a unique set of activities. The same is true for the regional organizations of the larger federal departments. The Region 8 organization of the Department of Housing and Urban Development is not a carbon copy of other parts of the larger system. It does its own thing, so to speak, and therefore it is worth examining as a separate organization for many research purposes.

But note that the regional organizations don't have an ordinary horizontal link with their national offices. They can't just switch their affiliation and move to another department even if that would seem desirable. There is still an *authority* relation, as a vertical link between the regional organization and the national organization. It is comparable to a city fire department which is quite autonomous in many ways but is still under the general control of city council. We can see, therefore, that if we examine the links which many organizations have, many of them are enmeshed in networks made up of numerous vertical links. And that is the case for more than governmental organizations. Note the vertical links implied in the following listing of subsidiaries of the Beatrice Foods Company.[1]

A holding and operating company, having on February 28, 1972 the following subsidiaries in which it had 100% voting power, except as indicated.

1. *Moody's Industrial Manual*, vol. 1 (New York: Moody's Investor's Services, Inc., 1973): 745-46.

Name and place of incorporation

Acme Die Casting Corp., Ill.
American Graphics Corp., Ill.
AGC/TV, Inc., Ill.
A. T. Supply, Inc., N.Y.
Aunt Nellie's Foods, Inc., Wisc.
Beatrice Foods Co., R.I.
Beatrice Disc. Inc., Del.
Beatrice Scientific Co., Del.
Brammer Enterprises, Inc., Fla.
Terminal Refrigerating Co., Cal.
Stahl Chemicals, S.A., Inc., Mass.
Russell Creamery Co. of
   Wisconsin, Inc.
Caravanner Insurance, Inc., Calif.
Charles Knitting, Inc., N.Y.
Chateau Mobile Homes, Fla.
County Line Cheese Co., Inc., Ind.
Cover Corp. of America, Del.
Crown Mold, Inc., Ill.
Everain Industries, Inc., N.J.
Golden Cookie Co., Mass.
Haul-Away, Inc., O.
I. E., Inc., Fla.
James J. Gallery, Inc., Mass.
E. W. Kneip, Inc., Ill.
Mantecados Payco, Inc., Del.
Marketing Communicators, Inc., Del.
Martha Lynden, Inc., Ill.
Mercury Screw Co., Ill.
Molub-Alloy Export, Ltd., Nev.
Morgan Yacht Corp., Fla.
North East Cold Storage Corp., Me.
Ocelot Sales, Inc., N.Y.

Overland Sales, Mass., Fla., Mich.,
   N.Y., Del., Conn., N.J., Pa., S.C.
Overland Yankee, Inc., Mich.
Pepcol Manufacturing Co., Colo.
Peter Eckrich & Sons, Inc., Del.
Pfister & Vogel Western Hemisphere,
   Inc., Del.
Primrose Corp., Ill.
Quincy Market Cold Storage &
   Warehouse Co., Mass.
Royal Crown Beverage Co., Del.
Royal Crown Bottling Co., Del.
Royal Crown Cola Bottling Co., Del.
Russell Creamery Co., Wisc.
San Lorenzo Corp., Del.
Seminole Metals, Inc., Fla.
Specialty Foods, Inc., Wisc.
Spiegel Industries Corp., N.J.
Stahl Chemicals S.A., Mass.
Striker Aluminum Yachts, Inc., Fla.
TTCI Liquidating Corp. (Formerly Treat
   Co., Inc.) N.Y.
Terminal Refrigerating Co., Calif.
Tip Top Brush Co., N.J.
Vatco Products Inc., Mass.
Vatco Sales & Services Co., Mass.
Zachary Confections, Inc., Ill.
Acabados Stahl de Mexico, S.A., Mexico
Acabados Neward, S.A., Mexico
Alphser, S.A., France
V. A. Armstrong & Son (Holdings)
   Pty. Ltd., Australia
Asunto Carimba, Guat.

Avondale Dairy Ltd., Canada
Aylmer Dairy Ltd., Canada
Aux Planteurs Reunis, S.A.,
  Switzerland
Beatrice-Australia Pty., Ltd., Australia
Beatrice Foods (U.K.) Ltd.,
  United Kingdom
Beneke Industries Ltd., Canada
Bireley's California Orange
  (Thailand) Ltd., Thailand (88%)
Bloomfield Industries Canada Ltd.,
  Canada
Brookside-Price's Dairy, Ltd., Canada
Brookside-Price's Dairy (Trente-Quinte)
  Ltd., Ont., Canada
Chemotechnik GmbH, West Germany
Cie Lacsoons, S.A., Belgium
Colonial Cookies, Ltd., Canada
Converters Ink Co. (Canada) Ltd.
Cremo Ltd., Jamaica (65%)
Crescent Creamery Ltd., Manitoba, Can.
Cryo-Diffusion S.A., France (84.6%)
Dairyworld S.A., Switzerland
Distribuidora Erics, Inc., P.R.
Elnagh S.p.A., Italy
Eric's Swiss Products, Inc., P.R.
Etahlissements Baud Societe Anonyme,
  France (75%)
Eurogum-Kaugummi GmbH & Co. K.G.,
  West Germany
Allibert Beneke Et Cie France (50%)
Artic, S.A., Belgium (50%)
Artic Nederland N.V., Holland
Artigel GmbH, West Germany
Beatrice & Motta, S.p.A., Italy (50%)
Beatrice Foods Sdn. Berhad Malaya
  (50%)
Beatrice Foods (Singapore) Ltd.,
  Singapore (50%)
Beatrice Scandinavia A/S, Norway (50%)
Bianca, S.A., Belgium (50%)
Die Hahn Food Industry Ltd., Korea (50%)
Glacieres & Frigoriferes De
  Chatelet, S.A., Belgium
Iceberg, S.A., Belgium
Polco, S.A., Belgium
S.A.L.P.A., S.A., Spain (50%)
Sodiereme, S.A.R.L., France (81.5%)
Eurocandy-Susswaren GmbH & Co.,
  K.G., West Germany
Europe Confectionary Co., Pty. Ltd.,
  Australia

Exthene (Holdings) Pty. Ltd., Australia
Exthene (Industrial) Pty. Ltd., Australia
Exthene (Victoria) Pty. Ltd., Australia
Eurocandy-Susswaren GmbH,
  West Germany
Fabrica de Brohas Perfect, S.A., de C.V.,
  Mexico
Fabrica de Dulces Gran Colombia S.A.,
  Colombia
Fabrica de Productos Alimenticios Rene
  S.A., (Guatemala) (70%)
Foods & Services A.G., Switzerland
Finance Corporation of Jamaica, Ltd.,
  Jamaica (65%)
De Forenede Isvaerker A/S, Denmark
  (75%)
Frigor C. Por A., Dominican Republic
  (70%)
Gelati Sanson, S.p.A., Italy (70%)
Goodysales Ltd., Jamaica
Hacienda La Rosita S.A., Costa Rica
Haco-Argento, Netherlands
Hancocks Golden Crust, Pty., Ltd.,
  Australia
N.V. Handelsvereeniging A.J. ten
  Doesschate, Netherlands (65%)
R. L. Haynes Pty., Ltd., Australia
Henry Berry & Co. (Australia) Ltd.,
  Australia
Henry Berry (Asian Region) Pty., Ltd.,
  Australia
Hijos de Ybarra, S.A., Spain
Holanda S.A., Mexico
Holmes Dairy Ltd., Ontario, Canada
Chicago Specialty Manufacturing of
  Canada Ltd.
Ideal Dairy Products Ltd., Canada
I.G.F.S., S.A., France
Interglas, S.A., Spain
Jack's Snacks de Colombia S.A.,
  Colombia
Laboratorios Farmaceuticos Gran
  Colombia S.A., Colombia
Lakeland Dairies, Ltd., Ontario, Canada
Lakeview Pure Milk Dairy Ltd., Canada
Malcolm Condensing Co. Ltd., Canada
Maple Lane Dairy Ltd., Canada
Market Forge of Canada, Ltd., Canada
Mecan, S.A. de C.V., Mexico
Melnor Manufacturing Ltd., Canada
Metallic Lubricants Ltd., Canada
Minigrip (Converting) Pty. Ltd.,

Australia
Minigrip (Australasia) Pty. Ltd.,
 Australia
Modernas Aplicaciones De La
 Refrigeracion Industrial, S.A.,
 Spain (88%)
Modern Dairies Ltd., Canada
Modern Dairies (Flin-Flon) Ltd.,
 Manitoba, Canada
Mow Sang Food Co., Ltd., Canada
Mr. Whippy Espana, S.A., Spain
Nippon Anchor, K.K., Japan
Northshore Dairies Ltd., Jamaica
O. K. Kaugummi, E. A. Walter Schumann
 K. G., West Germany
Oxford Dairy (Woodstock) Ltd., Canada
Patra Holdings Pty. Ltd., Australia
Polyvinyl Chemie (Holland), N.V.,
 Holland
Potato Distributors Ltd., Ireland
Premier Ls A/S, Denmark
Productos Chipy, S.A., Peru (85%)
Pyramid Homes (Eastern) Ltd., Canada
Pyramid Mobile Homes (1959) Ltd.,
 Canada
Pyramid Mobile Homes (Maritimes) Ltd.,
 Canada
Pyramid Mobile Homes (Saskatchewan)
 Ltd., Canada
Quan S.A. de C.V., Mexico
Quimica Stahl Centroamerica S.A.,
 Nicaragua (90%)
Red Tulip Chocolates Proprietary Ltd.,
 Australia

Reynolds & Company Pty. Ltd., Australia
St. Boniface Creamery Ltd., Manitoba,
 Canada
Sanna Dairies Ltd., Canada
Sedipro, S.A., France (75%)
Smith's Dairy Ltd., Canada
South Australian Scale Co. Pty. Ltd.,
 Australia
S.P.R.I. Imperial S.A.R.L., France
Stahl Chemicals (G.B.) Ltd.,
 United Kingdom
Stahl Chemische Industrien, N.V.,
 Netherlands
Stahl-Polyvinyl Chemie GmbH,
 West Germany
Stahl Finish (Canada) Ltd., Canada
Stahl Iberica, S.A., Spain
Stahl Polyvinyl International,
 Netherlands
Standard Dairies Ltd., Manitoba, Canada
Stark's Proprietary, Ltd., Australia
Stoffel y Cia., S.A., Mexico
Stratford & Frank Pty. Ltd., Australia
Striker Boats International Ltd., Bahamas
Tayto Ltd., Ireland (75%)
Tribol Schmierstoffe GmbH, Germany
Vogel Peterson (Canada) Ltd., Ont.,
 Canada
V-H Quality Food Products, Ltd., Canada
W. W. Weber Ltd., Canada
Wilmots Dairy Ltd., Canada
World Dryer, Ltd., Canada
Zuiveleentrale, Belgium

There are two general types of control which are usually represented in a vertical link between organizations. The first and perhaps most basic form of control deals with the budgeting process. The second form entails the setting of policy which must be followed.

If the superordinate or "higher" organization exercises control only over the major segments of the budget such as capital improvements and labor costs, we say that the subordinate or "lower" organization still has a large measure of autonomy. We can see a case which is in sharp contrast to that, how-ever, in the budgetary control exerted by the Office of Management and Budget in the Executive Office of the President during the Nixon administration. According to the reports of some administrators of Federal agencies the typical scenario went like this.

About mid-summer each agency was told to present the general outline of its proposed budget to the Office of Management and Budget (OMB). One or a few individuals within OMB then examined the budget to see if it reflected the policies and emphases and, above all, the total size that was in keeping with the President's preferences.

The written justification for each program within the agency budget was examined. If OMB, which sometimes meant a single powerful individual within OMB, did not approve a proposed new program or the continuation of an established program, the agency was told that there was inadequate justification for it, and the proposed budget should be changed accordingly. Some mild form of negotiation was permitted, but it was clear that OMB had the power to win any serious disagreements.

During the fall, each agency was required to submit its "final" proposed budget at which time OMB might make further deletions, or rarely, additions. All of the OMB approved proposed budgets were finally packaged into one big budget which the President sent to Congress early in the new year.

Next, both Houses of Congress held hearings during which agency officials were asked to explain, defend, and justify various relevant parts of the President's proposed budget. After the hearings, in due time, both the House and the Senate took action on the budgets which now might be slightly or even drastically different from what OMB proposed to Congress. Since the House and Senate versions of any agency's budget usually differ, there are negotiations conducted in what is called a Conference Committee. When the committee completes its work, the revised agency budget must be acted on by both Houses again. When finally passed the budget goes to the President. He might veto it, in which case the Congressional effort begins anew.

Now, if the President signed the bill you might think that finally an agency head would know how much money is available for each program. No such luck. An agency head might be told that further considera-

tion was being given by OMB to expenditures and some weeks or even months might pass before final budget decisions were made. In some cases it would be halfway through a new fiscal year before the agency would receive final budget information.

When the word did come, the budget might be changed only a little or markedly. The agency might receive "policy guidance" from OMB. The guidance might include the word that a whole program was being deleted and being transferred to another agency or dropped altogether. The funding for another program might be reduced by 50 percent and policy guidance given on how the program should be run. And these "after-the-fact" alterations applied even to programs and funding levels that had been approved by OMB before the budget was sent to Congress!

The withholding by the President of funds appropriated by Congress is called impounding. The agency heads as employees of the government can't very well take their "boss" to court but some citizen's groups and several states have done so and in a few cases the court has ordered the President to release the appropriated funds. But court action often takes many months if not years and during that time the agency has to try to carry one.

Clearly, the OMB, as the right arm of the President, was trying to enlarge its domain. It is most obvious with respect to Congress. With only a few minor exceptions in the past, the pattern of who should do what had been clear. "The President proposes and the Congress disposes," was the saying with regard to budgetary matters. There apparently had been consensus with regard to the domain of each.

But these events also represented an attempted change in the OMB domain vis-a-vis the Federal agencies. Before, it had been simply understood that when the President finally signed an appropriations bill or when Congress passed one over the President's veto, the overall budget for an agency was settled. The decision had been made. But now the OMB was trying to enlarge its domain by keeping each agency on the string, so to speak.

But as we noted in Chapter III, changing of an organization's domain involves negotiation. In this instance some of the negotiating was being done in court. And it is likely that some was going on behind the scenes between representatives of the White House and key Congressional leaders.

We have given you this detail on the budgetary process to help you understand something about what a vertical link between organizations might entail. The budgetary process in public or private organizations isn't always as complicated as the description suggests and certainly doesn't always involve such after the fact, capricious decisions, but often that possibility is there. Control over budget is a rather powerful handle, isn't it?

It should be clear that control over budget may also mean considerable control over organizational policy matters. But there are instances where the higher organization does not have any direct control over budget but does attempt to set general policies for the lower organization. They represent the second form of control mentioned earlier. This policy setting provides more autonomy for the lower organization. Policies are expressed in words and paragraphs and therefore are open to somewhat differing interpretation. There are usually several different ways to implement a policy and the managers of the lower organizations have some room for maneuvering so that the organization can do more nearly what they want it to do. Examples include some church congregations affiliated with a national organization or denomination,[2] universities belonging to an athletic conference such as the "Big 8" and hospitals wishing to be accredited by the American Hospital Association.

DEALINGS WITH OTHERS

We have seen that modern society is composed in part of networks of organizations with both horizontal and vertical links. Let's conclude by examining the day-to-day dealings of two kinds of organizations: Banks and meat processing plants. We could have used any two organizations. There is nothing especially unusual about these two.

Any bank or other organization has what is called an *organization set*.[3] The set is composed of those other organizations that make a difference for the one that we are focusing our attention on. We will call it the focal organization. The focal organization has a number of other organizations with which there is reasonably regular interaction. They make up a large part of the organization set. In addition, there are other organizations such as competitors where regular and direct interaction may be infrequent, but where the actions of the other organizations are taken into consideration within the focal organization. These significant other organizations are also part of the organization set.

2. James R. Wood, "Authority and Controversial Policy: The Churches and Civil Rights" *American Sociological Review* 35 (Dec., 1970): 1057-1069.

3. William M. Evan, "The Organization Set: Toward a Theory of Interorganizational Relations," in *Approaches to Organizational Design,* ed., James D. Thompson, (Pittsburgh, Penn.: University of Pittsburgh Press, 1966), 173-188.

Using a bank and a meat processing plant, let's examine the components of an organization set.

Most organizations have *suppliers* in their organization set. It is a rare organization that includes all the raw materials, products, services, personnel, and ideas which it uses entirely within the organization. There are usually a number of other organizations which provide *input* to the focal organization. The meat processing plant gets input from the stockyards, manufacturers of large equipment, and packaging materials, and the wholesalers of such things as tools and office supplies. An employment agency or the state employment service may be called on from time to time to provide applicants for job vacancies in the plant. Numerous other input organizations could be mentioned.

But what are the inputs to a bank? In addition to the necessary paper products, heating fuel, equipment, personnel, and new ideas, to name just a few, there is that basic ingredient called money. Some of it comes from individuals and corporate sources in the form of savings. Some of it comes in from interest on loans and profit from investments of many kinds. But even with these income sources, the bank would be in difficulty if it was not able to draw on the many reserves of Federal Reserve Banks from time to time. The bank borrows money from the Federal Reserve so that we will be able to secure a loan from the local bank to pay for our car.

In any organization set, you will usually find those persons and organizations called *customers or clients*. The processing plant would normally have less than a dozen customers such as meat products wholesalers to whom its products are sold. The bank, on the other hand, has several thousand cus-

tomers ranging from large corporations, small businesses, to individuals. The bank offers a range of services to its customers while the meat processing plant has a limited range of products to sell to customers.

Not all organizations have obvious *competitors* but the bank and processing plant do. The meat plant may not have much regular interaction with other similar plants, but there is likely to be an acute awareness of the selling process and buying and selling policies of competitors. One of the interesting aspects of lively, real competition as contrasted to pseudocompetition is the extent and ways in which organizations go about monitoring their environments, especially the activities and plans of their competitors. Actually the officials of the plant have an arena for learning what their competitors are up to, at least in part, because their buyers go to the same stockyards and bid against the buyers of the competing firms. What they pay and the apparent quality of what they buy is open to everyone in most instances.

Who are the bank's competitors? There may be more of them than you might expect. In addition to other banks, both commercial and industrial, there are the savings and loan associations. The latter do not offer all of the same services but there is considerable overlap. Then there are the small finance companies which may be able to give you a loan from a few hundred dollars up to perhaps $50,000. They specialize in higher interest rates for higher risk loans. In addition there are some mortgage and finance companies which specialize in real estate, retail businesses which cash payroll and personal checks, and more recently, some nonbanking establishments which offer the sale of traveler's cheques. Stockbrokerage firms offer alternatives for investment as do real estate brokers. Even the U. S. Postal Service will sell you a postal money order which competes with a bank draft.

Many of the basic banking services that may be offered are regulated by one or more governmental agencies and that regulation precludes many forms of competition that might otherwise take place. That regulation also requires that information on interest rates and types of loans, for example, be readily available to anyone. However, information about specific loans and investments is often guarded with great care by the bank officials. Therefore, if the competitors of our bank want that kind of information, they must go to the trouble of ferreting it out from some of the other persons or organizations involved in the transaction.

A good deal of the competition in banking services seems to center on: 1) the cleverness and persistence of advertising campaigns and, 2) the pleasantness and convenience of the services rendered. Whether or not the advertising efforts make much difference is not clear since usually all of the competitors within an area engage in advertising.

Our local bank has almost daily interaction with its competitors. After all, it cashes checks which have been written on dozens of other banks and if it wants to get its money back the exchanges must become routinized.

Whether the plant and bank officials would prefer it that way or not, there are also *regulators*, outside agencies established by law, to promulgate and enforce rules which are supposed to make things more predictable and safe.

Almost all businesses and public buildings are checked periodically by the local fire department inspectors for any possible violation of fire safety regulations. Our meat processing plant is inspected regularly by the local health department and the U. S. Department of Agriculture Inspectors examine the quality of meat being processed if any of the products are going to be involved in interstate commerce.

Banks probably are subject to more scrutiny than any other enterprise in our society. In the past and even occasionally today, you will hear of a bank "failure." Sometimes that may mean that the bank, as with any other business operation, has gotten into a hole when its debts far exceed its assets. In earlier generations if the word got around that the bank was in trouble, many customers would quickly withdraw their deposits thus assuring that the banking operation would collapse. Now that "run on the bank" phenomenon has been largely stopped. A Federal Deposit Insurance Corporation was set up specifically to insure that no depositor would lose his money even if a bank were poorly managed. Currently, deposits up to $20,000 are so insured.

Handling other people's money even where elaborate record keeping is a standard procedure seems to offer overwhelming temptation to some people. Cressey found that persons who hold positions of financial trust and later embezzle funds first went through a period of rationalizing that behavior by convincing themselves that they were only borrowing the money and that no one really would be hurt.[4]

In an effort to preclude embezzlement or other misuse of bank funds, inspection procedures have been set up.

4. Donald R. Cressey, *Other People's Money: A Study in the Social-psychology of Embezzlement* (Belmont, Calif.: Wadsworth Publishing Company, 1953: Rep. 1971).

Finally, our two organizations have *allies* at certain times. Even competitors become close allies when the threat is thought to be great. When the state or Federal government propose additional controls, officials of all banks whether competitors or not, are likely to join together to stop it or to make the outcome more acceptable. On occasion, banks in a community will work together and refuse to provide the necessary capital for some proposed large-scale development which they don't like. The most common occurence, of course, is where banks and the officials of other business enterprises work together to try to attract new industry to their area. Until recently at least, it was simply assumed that economic and population growth were extremely desirable and anyone who questioned that concept was said to be at least a troublemaker. Now at least on occasion, a few bankers and other business leaders are beginning to recognize that growth brings with it many undesirable consequences as well. In a few rare cases in the United States, bankers and their allies have worked together to try to reduce the rate of growth or to maintain a stable population and economy. For example, in 1972, Santa Fe, New Mexico decided *not* to enlarge its airport even though the decision makers knew that saying "no" would mean the cessation of commercial airline service to the city. But that type of action is a very rare event in the United States except for a few unique communities.

And our meat plant has allies also at times. As in any segment of industry and commerce where similar business enterprises frequently provide advice and support to each other when there are such things as confrontations with labor unions or with proposed new government regulations, our plant officials arrange for coali-tions with other similar organizations when the chips are down. Further, this focal organization probably contributes some money to one or a few national associations that claim to represent its interests in Congress and with relevant agencies such as the Federal Trade Commission. In fact, this banning together in an attempt to influence either the government or the general consumer market is so common that it is rare that any focal organization isn't allied with its competitors through one or more such associations.

This topic anticipates the theme of the next chapter: How the environments of organizations vary and what it means for organizational autonomy, security, and prestige.

For Further Reading

Aldrich, Howard E. "Organizational Boundaries and Inter-organizational Conflict." *Human Relations*, 24 (August, 1971), pp. 279-282.

Different types of organizations, or populations as Aldrich calls them, have different environments in part because they are hooked into different networks.

Evan, William M. "The Organizational Set: Toward a Theory of Interorganizational Relations." *Approaches to Organizational Design*. Edited by James D. Thompson, Pittsburgh: University of Pittsburgh Press, 1966.

Taking the earlier notion of role set, Evan shows how the normative structure requires each organization to conduct repeated interaction with a limited set of other organizations.

Heydebrand, Wolf V., ed. *Comparative Organizations: The Results of Empirical Research*. Englewood Cliffs, N.J.: Prentice-Hall, 1973.

This book contains 30 articles dealing with many different kinds of organizations ranging from business firms, health, welfare, and educational organizations to voluntary organizations. Contains excellent source material. Most of the articles are reprinted from scholarly journals.

Moore, Wilbert E. *The Conduct of the Corporation*. New York: Random House, 1962.

Some straight talk which should dispell some common notions about how corporations are rational, efficient systems for the maximization of profit for the investors.

Turk, Herman. "Interorganizational Networks in Urban Society: Initial Perspectives and Comparative Research." *American Sociological Review*, 35 (February, 1970), pp. 1-19.

This is an intriguing study of the flow of poverty funds from Federal agencies to and among organizations within the 130 largest United States cities.

Warren, Ronald L. "The Interorganizational Field as a Focus for Investigation." *Administrative Science Quarterly*, 12 (December, 1967), pp. 396-419.

A look at the joint concerns and actions of "community decision organizations" in Philadelphia, Detroit, and Boston. Includes study of community welfare councils, urban renewal authorities, chambers of commerce, federations of churches, municipal health and welfare departments, boards of education, and so on.

6 | Environmental Variations

WHEN you drive through some of the working class suburbs around a large city you may see block after block of houses that appear to be almost carbon copies of each other. And at a superficial level, many of the families living in those houses may appear to be very much like each other. One might erroneously conclude that each child is growing up in the same environment.

Even short-term observation would reveal that what a child experiences in one family is very different from what another experiences in his family setting. Both families may consist of two parents in their early thirties and children aged 5 and 9 years, but there may be a very high level of tension and mutual mistrust in one family and the very opposite in the other.

Similarly two organizations such as two schools, two church congregations, or two engineering firms may be located in the same community. Each pair may have about the same number of members and be about the same age but the significant segments of their environments as experienced may be very different. One engineering firm may have a reputation for doing very competent and very expensive work and therefore has a small but very loyal clientele while the other firm does barely adequate but less

expensive work which means that a significant proportion of its customers don't come back a second time. Thus, the second firm has to scramble for new business almost all of the time. Its environment isn't exactly hostile but neither is the firm very benevolent. Just as no two organizations have identical internal characteristics, it is even more the case that their respective environments vary markedly.

While it is interesting and challenging to try to understand the internal dynamics of organizations it is even more challenging to try to make sense of organization-environment dynamics.

We have already discussed one major component of any organization's environment, its horizontal and vertical links to other organizations. Let's now examine briefly some of the broad, abstract dimensions of organization-environment interaction.

Within any single organization some groups can influence and control other groups in rather significant ways. To what extent is that also true in the pushing and shoving that goes on between an organization and significant elements in its environment?

84

HASSLES WITH THE ENVIRONMENT

Organizations are social systems. Most organizations got started because someone or a collection of persons developed some ideas and planned the official normative structure and, at least to some extent, the resource structure of the organization. But after it was born, so to speak, it developed and changed in a variety of ways at least some of which were unplanned and perhaps even unanticipated by the managers or owners. To a very significant degree, it seems that an organization once started, grows, changes, and takes on a momentum of its own.[1] Organizations do vary, of course, in the number and kinds of goals or missions that are listed in official pronouncements but you should not be surprised to learn that organizations with identical official goals may be quite dissimilar internally and relate to their environments in quite disparate ways. The variation is especially obvious for those organizations which are intended to "make profit for the owners." So what are different organizations really up to? How do we make sense of organization-environment interaction?

One useful way is to start by noting that organizations appear to be striving for autonomy, security, and prestige just as groups do within an organization.[2] While both officials and nonofficials of an organization may have a variety of motivations for what they do as organizational participants, when we step back and look at the organization as a whole and examine the various hassles with environmental units, it appears that there is something going on much like a continuous struggle by the organization to maintain or increase its *autonomy, security,* and *prestige.* A good deal of this struggle can be observed in the negotiations that go on with respect to the organization's *domain.* We shall try to illustrate these notions as we move along.

A few organizations seem to dominate, indeed almost overwhelm, their environments. Examples are the Department of Defense, International Telephone and Telegraph (ITT), and General Motors Corporation. Many organizations, particularly small ones, seem to be at the opposite extreme. They are on the verge of being overwhelmed by their environments. Many organizations are dissolved or simply cease to function each year. Small business firms are a prime example. But most organizations fall between these two extremes.

What are some of the "power means" which organizations sometimes use to cope with various environmental units? Coercion or the threat of coercion is used infrequently. Occasionally disputes develop between labor unions and management which lead to long, bitter strikes which evolve into coercive action such as bombing or physical threats against persons. A more common power means is the threat or use of unfavorable publicity. Apparently both Ralph Nader's organization and General Motors have tried to use this technique on each other. The threat or the actual withholding of critically needed products or services can bring desired results under certain circumstances. This, of course, is why the strike can be a very effective weapon. Bribes and kickbacks which seem to go along with large public works projects with disgusting regularity give the "successful" organizations at

1. Philip Selznick, *TVA and the Grass Roots* (Berkeley and Los Angeles: University of California Press, 1949).
2. J. Eugene Haas and Thomas E. Drabek, *Complex Organizations: A Sociological Perspective.* (New York: Macmillan, 1973), pp. 175-202.

least a temporary advantage. The judicious use of favors can promote a sense of obligation for possible future use. Thus, if my organization goes out of its way to do several favors for your organization now, that subsequent obligation increases my organization's autonomy and security in the future. It gives my organization a bit more control over its environment.

Where several organizations get together to fix prices or arrange for restrictions of supplies, they gain an advantage over the rest of their competitors. Most such collusive agreements are illegal in the United States but in all probability are quite widespread anyway.

In the 1972 Presidential election, the various groups and committees working for the reelection of President Nixon had almost twice as much money available for advertising, travel, and publicity in general as did those working for his opponent. Effective use of resources to influence significant others by means of advertising, lobbying activities and the like can provide a very significant basis for dominating certain segments of the environment.

We should not, of course, overlook interpersonal influence. A principal reason why many executives belong to service clubs such as Lions and Kiwanis is to increase the number of their acquaintances and friends. This allows them to handle more interorganizational matters on a more personal basis than would otherwise be the case.

And finally there is the power means mentioned earlier—authority. One major reason why many governmental organizations can get their way is that there is general consensus that they have a legal right and even an obligation to do so. Many executives might prefer that the Internal Revenue Service (IRS) not examine the financial records of their organizations but only a few such persons would seriously dispute the authority of the IRS to do so. Managers and owners of business firms have not been elated with the price controls developed by the federal government but only a handful have challenged the right of the government to enact and enforce such controls. It can be seen then that organizations which have an authority basis for their attempts to influence and control key environmental units have a higher level of organizational security than those which must rely mostly on other power means.

Quite apart from the specific means used, some organizations are more opportunistic than others.[3] *Opportunism* is the practice of adapting the organization's actions to immediate and short-term circumstances without regard to basic organizational character or long-range consequences. It is the, "we will do business with anybody so long as we can make a profit," attitude. Examples include a school which changes its curriculum every time a new fad develops,[4] a business firm which will take on any new product for sale without checking on future availability of the product or the possibility of maintenance services and parts for repair which the customers might need, and a city government which encourages and even offers large tax incentives and land to potential new industries without any serious examination of the probable effects of such industries on the character of the community as a whole, the consequences to the

3. For a more detailed discussion of how organizations may relate to their environments, see *Ibid.*, pp. 207-214.
4. Burton R. Clark, *Adult Education in Transition: A Study of Institutional Insecurity* (Berkeley and Los Angeles: University of California Press, 1956).

physical environment and on the tax burden to its future citizens.

Some more conservative organizations take such actions only after careful and thorough attempts to examine longer range consequences. For them opportunism is thought to be a threat to the organization's prestige and security. But for other organizations opportunism is viewed as the key to survival.

Some organizations are noted for their *activism*. They probe, monitor, and attempt to manipulate their environmental units more thoroughly and consistently than do most organizations. Some corporations and associations have full-time, paid, lobbyists and information seekers. Their jobs are to be on top of all relevant events and to relay that information promptly to the organization's managers and in some organizations, to the members in general. An activist organization ordinarily puts a larger proportion of its resources into advertising or other sales techniques than do most organizations of its type. Some religious organizations and national associations are clearly more activist than others. And when the more activist organizations attempt to work in concert with those who are less so, the ensuing tension and conflict can become intense.[5] Law and medical firms are forbidden by professional standards to advertise but most other forms of activism are still open to them.

Economic considerations would suggest that the very poor organization which is barely making ends meet probably can't afford the added cost of a high level of activism. When there is a recession, one of the first adjustments that many business firms make is a quick reduction in the programs to monitor and manipulate the environment.

Another dimension which deserves attention is the environmental base for continuity and certainty of support for the organization. Even under a wide range of possible circumstances it is hard to imagine that certain organizations won't continue to exist into the indefinite future. Consider the following organizations: Court system, public school, electric power company, department of highway maintenance, prison, postal service organization, and an airport authority. The domains of organizations such as these are relatively clear-cut and generally approved by all interested parties. The view on all sides seems to be that the service or product which each organization supplies is so basic and the demand for it so consistent that somehow or other the organization must be kept alive and functioning.

Each of these organizations is at least in one sense a monopoly. Each exists in a very *benevolent* rather than a *hostile environment*. Each has what might be called maximum security in its relations with most of its environmental segments. Its survival is not really in doubt. It is analogous to an organization which holds a large number of patents for products which are in very high demand now and will continue to be so for many decades into the future. The dependency of environmental units on the organization's product or service is almost total and, as a result, the organization is extremely secure.

But you should not assume that such a secure organization necessarily has a high degree of autonomy or prestige. Many secure organizations are closely regulated which means that their autonomy is low. Others, such as the police department, may

5. James R. Wood, "Authority and Controversial Policy: The Churches and Civil Rights," *American Sociological Review* 53 (Dec. 1970): 1057-1069.

be granted relatively little prestige despite the organization's security.

There are other organizations whose survival is continuously in jeopardy. For example, the Black Panthers, American Nazi Party, Youth International Party, and to a lesser degree, nudist associations, all find that it is frequently difficult to find the space, financing, and "fair" news coverage, for example, which most other organizations can almost take for granted.

So while some organizations "have it made" so to speak, for others it is often not at all clear how long they can survive in a hostile environment. But note that even secure organizations may be subject to external demands and pressures. The U. S. Postal Service is frequently being criticized for not delivering the mail fast enough and not having the post office open longer hours. Various pressure groups in the local area frequently hassle the school board and the superintendent about adding their favorite subject or program to the school curriculum.

Let's examine this and other issues as we look briefly at the environment of a city police department.

STRUCTURED ENVIRONMENTAL CONSTRAINTS

A city police department is a paramilitary organization. That is, it has an internal authority structure and a training program which stresses strict obedience, rapid physical mobility of individual members or small units, and frequent use of coercion or the threat thereof. What is more, such a police organization has a clearly defined turf. It is responsible for "law enforcement" within a designated geographical area, usually within the city limits.

It is a very secure organization in the sense that every United States city has a police department and it is almost inconceivable that one would ever be disbanded. The organization will be there five years from now come "hell or high water." If we review the structured environmental constraints within which the police organizations exist, however, we will learn that despite its paramilitary character, it seldom runs roughshod over many of its environmental components.

Figure 6.1 is an actual organizational chart for a city of 85,000 population. A chart of this type is designed to list all of the principal components of the city government and to indicate by the display of lines between boxes the nature of the normatively prescribed relation between the components. Thus the line between the City Manager and the police, fire, administrative services, etc., departments is intended to indicate that the City Manager operating within the policies and rules set up by the City Council is authorized to direct and review the work and the policies of the eight departments shown on that line. They are what we call the *line* departments. The Assistant to the City Manager and the Economic and Fiscal Policy Advisor, however, are what we call *staff*. Note also that the City Attorney's office is controlled by and reports directly to the City Council rather than to the City Manager.

The lines also indicate that any desired or necessary coordination of plans and activities among and between the various line departments is the responsibility of the City Manager's office. At least that is the way the organizational chart indicates it is supposed to take place.

Coordination of effort within a department is to be directed by the head of the department. Thus, for example, the Office of the Chief of Police is supposed to see to it that

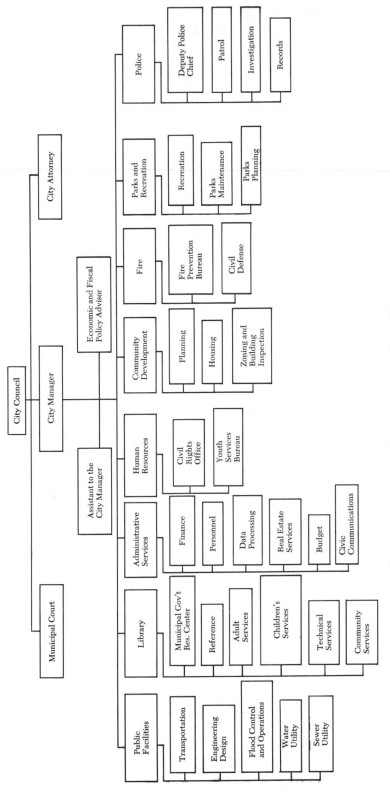

Figure 6.1., Principal Components of Small City Government

the needed coordination among the Patrol, Investigation, and Records division is in fact carried out.

Now let's go a step further and fill in some details that might not be obvious from looking at the chart. We will use the term "police" to refer to the police department or police organization.

Now suppose that police officials note that the population within the city limits has been increasing and also that the crime rate has gone up. From the police perspective, one significant part of the environment has changed. An organization's environment may be viewed from different levels of abstraction. Here it is the characteristics of the community as a whole. At another level, the environment of the police consists of the other departments and offices which make up city government.

The police noting the increase in the population and crime rate may want to adapt by expanding the size of the patrol. The request would go to the City Manager's office where an initial decision would be made after reviewing comments on the proposed increase from the Finance, Personnel, and Budget sections of Administrative Services. And if the additional personnel were to need facilities not currently available, that would bring in Real Estate Services from Administrative Services and most of the components of the Public Facilities department. Also the Civil Rights office is likely to be involved. Comments and recommendations from these other parts of city government will have some impact on the City Manager's decision to recommend or not some proposed increase for consideration by the City Council. The City Council, in turn, will want to know such things as how the ratio of patrol officers per 1,000 population in this city compares with the ratio for

other cities of similar size. So even the actions of other City Councils, half-a-nation distant, may have an effect on whether or not our police can increase the size of its patrol!

Take another matter having nothing to do with growth. Suppose there is a large fire in the city with hundreds of spectators, cars jammed in the nearby streets, etc. Both police and fire units are likely to be there. Or suppose there is a civil disturbance with looting and firebombing in progress. Who is in charge in such cases? The City Manager or his representative can't be there to coordinate the efforts. Because of the spontaneous and dynamic nature of such situations, there have to be agreements in advance between the police and fire organizations if any effective coordination is going to exist when the big events come. So the police negotiate with the fire department about the potentially overlapping domains to establish which organization has the "lead" or primary decision-making authority for which kinds of events. The other organization then can follow up on those decisions made at the scene and supplement the primary effort. Doesn't sound too much like a free wheeling, autonomous paramilitary organization, does it?

But the need to negotiate, compromise and respond doesn't stop at the boundary of the system called city government. As you may have noted in the news reports in the last few years, there are outside groups and organizations which are very vocal and sometimes physically aggressive in their demands that police policies and domain be altered to suit their preferences. Some groups insist that the police "get tough with lawbreakers" while other groups demand an immediate stop to "police brutality." Much of this vocal disagreement centers on police handling of persons who have low ethnic or minority status such as Puerto Ricans, Blacks, American Indians, and Mexican Americans. Why should the police have to respond to and perhaps compromise with such vocal groups? They are usually a tiny minority of the total community. They seldom have a hammerlock on city council and its policies regarding the operation of the police department. Why don't police officials simply ignore all of the noise those groups make?

Do you remember the mention of unfavorable publicity as a power means? In many, but not all cities, the news media report such outcries. They find where violence has occurred between the police and citizens as especially newsworthy. Since the police are usually better trained in the use of and better armed for violence, it is the citizen who is most likely to get clobbered in the fray. Did the police use unnecessary force? Were the police just responding to the violence initiated by the citizen(s)? Usually the news reporters aren't on the scene when the violence erupts. They have to try to piece the story together from a number of eyewitnesses whose accounts often conflict. The reporter tries to present the whole story insofar as possible. This gives at least some credence to the police version of what happened as well as that of protesting groups. Thus time and again a controversy swirls around the police department. Police officials, city council members, and the mayor become concerned lest the image of the police become so tarnished that most citizens won't cooperate with them when needed. As conquering armies have learned over the centuries, a hostile, noncooperative population can make life almost unbearable for their would-be masters. Then it becomes very unsafe for a single police

patrolman to walk the beat alone. They must go everywhere in pairs which means that more police officers must be hired or less area patroled. City officials, especially elected officials, don't like either of those alternatives. And when there is a feeling on the part of some minority segment that the police can't or won't protect them adequately, vigilante groups are likely to arise; e.g., male homosexuals organized to protect themselves in San Francisco.[6] Such groups may threaten the domain of the police. They are in fact performing a type of police function.

Thus when there are charges of illegal or irregular behavior by police, top police officials are likely to take some action within the department to "correct the situation." The "corrective action" may be defined by the "get tough" crowd as just another example of tying the hands of policemen. The other side is likely to scream "whitewash." After that series of events is repeated a number of times, a typical solution is advanced and given wide publicity in the news media. Why not, say the "fair-minded" and often prominent members of the community, set up an impartial outside, civilian review board whose members will be selected for their common sense and fairmindedness. Then when a controversy arises the review board can "examine all of the facts" and reach a "balanced judgment" as to whether the police behaved appropriately or not. The findings, conclusions and recommendations, if any, can then be made public. If the top police officials and the city council wish to use the findings to formulate changes in police department policy or procedures so much the better. What

6. "The Lavender Panthers," *Time* 102:15 (Oct. 8, 1973), p. 73.

could be less threatening and more helpful to police-community relations than that?

Remember what was said about the continuous struggle to maintain and enhance organizational autonomy, security, and prestige? If that notion has any validity, what would you anticipate that the response of the police would be to a suggested civilian review board? Right! It would be one more interest group threat to the autonomy of the police organization. And its influence could well become powerful to the point where it might overshadow the City Council on certain policy matters. Have you ever heard serious demands for an outside review board for the engineering or fire department? If the police organization was the only organization to have such a review board, the implication would be clear: The police are untrustworthy, incompetent, or both, to handle their own affairs. Further, unless most of the "better" police departments in the country had similar review boards, our police department would see the proposed board as a threat to its prestige.

Sometimes such civilian review boards are forced on police departments at the expense of their autonomy and prestige. You can bet that every effort is made covertly to see that the board becomes a meaningless front or a tool of the police department to improve its image and shield the organization from other even less desirable encroachments on its autonomy and prestige.

There is another kind of encroachment on police organizations which we have seen develop in recent years. Just as nurses in some hospitals, elementary and secondary schoolteachers, and even college professors are becoming unionized, so too is the issue arising in police departments. The argument is straightforward enough. Police personnel have jobs which are sometimes dangerous, often boring, often requiring great interpersonal skill, sometimes requiring great courage. Because fringe benefits and salaries are inadequate, the persons who are attracted to police work are, in more than the usual proportions, sadistic and incompetent in many ways. Thus, the argument goes, we have these constant wars and armed truces between the police and large segments of the population. In larger cities, police corruption and ties with the underworld further aggravate the situation. Since the city fathers won't, the argument continues, correct the reward structure so that better quality persons will be attracted to police work, the only reasonable answer is to unionize the police and force the city fathers to change their position.

For many a police officer the reasoning is a bit different but the conclusion the same. He will say that the work is dangerous, demanding, and requires a great deal of skill. Therefore, police officers should receive pay and fringe benefits comparable to that received by those in other "professions."[7]

It isn't difficult to see why unionizing might be a threat to a police organization. For an organization whose image and normative structure are centered on the notion of unchallenged command and control, any organizational arrangement which would tend to make police personnel less responsive to the commands of higher officers is going to be anathema. If the union leaders call for a strike or a slow-down action and the majority of voting union members approve it, then the unionized police personnel have to decide *whose* decisions to follow—those

7. Commission on Educational Reconstruction, *Organizing the Teaching Profession: The Story of the American Federation of Teachers* (Glencoe, Ill.: Free Press, 1955).

of their police captains and lieutenants or those of the union. A police department may survive unionization but it will be a different organization thereafter and it will be less autonomous.

UPSETTING THE APPLECART

When an earthquake strikes a city there will be no time to do any last minute planning or mobilizing of emergency organizations. It all happens without notice. (Research is being conducted on earthquake forecasting however, and prediction may become feasible someday.) There will probably be some new tasks to perform such as rescuing the injured and the dead from collapsed buildings, but mostly the tasks will just be greatly increased in scope and urgency. And because the following will all develop at about the same time, the total demand on the responsible community organizations as a whole will be quantitatively and qualitatively different from normal. Large areas of the city will be without electric power, phone service will be nonexistent or unpredictable, there will be a few scattered fires at first and later there will be many more started from the ruptured gas lines. Water pressure will be available in some areas but not others, and the information will start to accumulate to suggest that the sewer system is broken in numerous places but it is not clear how many breaks and where they are. Massive traffic jams will occur and several major streets will be impassable due to fallen debris and dropped bridge spans. Getting emergency equipment to fires and badly damaged buildings becomes very difficult.

Now consider what changes, if any, will likely take place in the operation of relevant organizations in this earthquake-stricken city. Search and rescue groups will spring up without much, if any, prior planning; most organizations will try to get their usual operations going again through whatever means seem to make sense and are possible. Many off-duty organization members will show up at their job when they are reasonably sure that close family and friends are not in dire need of help.[8]

For many organizations this is a very unusual, almost novel situation that they are facing. Communication is bad and hard facts are very scarce. Nevertheless it appears to most members of an organization that the damage is massive, that their workload has exploded in size and complexity. Furthermore there is a sense of extreme urgency. Many temporary repairs must be made and emergency actions taken to reduce the likelihood that more persons will be killed and injured and more property damaged. And the victims must be given shelter, food, and comfort quickly. It seems like almost everything must be done at once.

Several changes in organizational functioning are likely to occur. Since the tasks that must be tackled immediately are spread all over the city, many lower level employees see things that must be corrected and work that must be done and they proceed to do it without checking with their bosses. Thus, many decisions which would normally be made at middle or upper levels of the organization are made at lower levels. What is more, because of the urgency to get on with the emergency work, few if any rec-

8. This varies somewhat depending on the culture. See, *The Great Alaska Earthquake of 1964: Human Ecology* (Washington, D.C.: Committee on the Alaska Earthquake, National Academy of Sciences, 1970), in contrast to Robert W. Kates, et al., "Human Impact of the Managua Earthquake Disaster" *Science* 182 (Dec. 7, 1973): 981-990.

ords are kept. This makes the settling of financial responsibilities very difficult later.

Because these lower level workers are dispersed about the city, getting word back to the central office or headquarters about what has been done and what still needs to be done is slow and problematic. Thus, top officials in each organization, e.g., public works department, civil defense, engineering department, have only a smattering of information about what needs to be done and is being done. Partially because of this dearth of information within any one organization and because there develops a strong conviction that some new means of coordinating the efforts of the various organizations is needed, some type of emergency operating center is quickly set up. Its principal intended functions are to collect and sort out fact from rumor and make this useful information available quickly to all responsible organizations and to coordinate the actions of all of the organizations so that duplication can be minimized and needed areas of effort won't be overlooked. This new organizational structure becomes a temporary "synthetic organization," an overarching organization placed above the regular operating organizations.[9] At the time this new super organization is formed it seems like an obvious and desirable requirement to most organizational officials and they tend to support it wholeheartedly at least for the first few days.

But when the environment changes, when the period of extreme urgency passes, the pressure to disband the coordinating center starts to build up quickly. Even though a good case could be made for the need to continue the coordinating center through the restoration and reconstruction periods, top officials find all sorts of reasons to give for disbanding it. Why? While each or-

ganization was willing to give up some autonomy for the sake of better overall coordination and therefore the good of the community during the height of the emergency, each organization now wants to reassert its autonomy. The general environment has changed and therefore the specific environment for each organization has also changed. Thus, once again the concern for continued or enhanced organizational autonomy, security, and prestige reemerges.

And who is to say that that concern is entirely undesirable? Would you want to work in an organization that was insecure, that was subject to the changing whims of other more powerful organizations, where the departments might be reorganized every few months? At least that would be a change from the inflexibility of the so-called typical bureaucratic organization which seems to be facing so many of us. That is the subject of our final chapter.

For Further Reading

Baldridge, J. Victor. *Power and Conflict in the University.* New York: John Wiley and Sons, Inc., 1971.

  A careful, thoughtful case study of a large metropolitan university. It shows in some detail how the internal dynamics of the organization were altered by external changes. Good illustration of concern for organizational prestige and autonomy.

Drabek, Thomas E. *Disaster in Aisle 13.* Columbus: College of Administrative Science, The Ohio State University, 1968.

  A detailed case study of how a devastating explosion at the Indianapolis, Indiana Coliseum suddenly changed the environment of

9. James D. Thompson and Robert W. Hawkes, "Disaster, Community Organization and Administrative Process," in *Man and Society in Disaster,* George W. Baker and Dwight Chapman, eds., (New York: Basic Books, Inc., 1962), pp. 268-300.

many organizations and of their response to that change.

Emery, F. E. and Trist, E. L. "Causal Texture of Organizational Environments." *Human Relations* 18 (February, 1965), pp. 21-32.

One of the earliest and most cited empirical works on organization-environment interaction.

Perrow, Charles. *Complex Organizations: A Critical Essay*. Glenview, Illinois: Scott, Foresman and Co., 1972.

An incisive and sometimes witty, short book which summarizes and dissects many of the theoretical perspectives on organizations. His discussion of what he calls the "institutional school" is especially helpful in understanding organizational environments.

Stinchcombe, Arthur L. "Social Structure and Organizations." *Handbook of Organizations*. Edited by James G. March. Chicago: Rand-McNally and Company, 1965, pp. 142-193.

Why do certain kinds of organizations arise, proliferate and prosper while others do not? Stinchcombe treats that and related questions by examining the broader societal setting within which organizations exist.

Thompson, James D. *Organization in Action*. New York: McGraw-Hill Book Company, 1967.

A tightly written volume by an experienced, wise author. His discussion of how organizations monitor and respond to the environment is perhaps the best to date.

Zald, Mayer. *Organizational Change: The Political Economy of the YMCA*. Chicago: University of Chicago Press, 1970.

Even the good, old "Y" has competitors and a changing environment. This case study provides a view of how the relevant environmental sectors appear through the eyes of the managers.

7 | Bureaucratic Death–Must That Be My Future

NOW let's return to you. What has all this to do with you? Does it mean anything more than a set of terms, definitions, and a few facts that you can memorize, regurgitate back on an examination, and quickly forget? Perhaps so! But we hope not. For our goal has been to stimulate you not only to think about large organizations and how they function, but about yourself, and most importantly, your future. What options do *you* have? Must you work in a large organization? And if you do, how will your life be affected?

THE LIVING DEAD

Some years ago, Franz Kafka wrote of a man who woke up one morning only to discover that he had been transformed into a large beetle.[1] Having gone to sleep on his back, he struggles desperately to try and turn over. Think of it—a beetle! Think of the fright that would accompany such a discovery. As you moved along methodically, think how you would fear that someone, totally beyond your power, might at any instant squash you all over the floor. And what could your parents do other than try to keep your transformation a secret.

Yet, look at the lives that many lead today. Recall our helicopter observation post? Watch them gulp a quick breakfast and rush to their jobs. Or do they really move with much zest? Oh, they get there alright, but it takes an effort. Here they sell their lives away doing as directed by their superiors, who also specify when and how much. But are they happy? Is there joy? Is there a sense of excitement? Anticipation? Accomplishment? Or have they resigned themselves to a distinction: Jobs are for making money, leisure for spending it.[2] And, if so, then wouldn't we expect persons to try in every way possible to maximize the time available for leisure? "When the two compete, leisure wins hands down."[3]

Recognizing this split and the hedonistic philosophy that has emerged for many Americans, Philip Roth has updated Kafka.[4] How? He replaced the beetle with a sensi-

1. Franz Kafka, *The Metamorphosis*, trans. Willa and Edwin Muir (New York: Schocken Books, 1968; original publication, 1935).
2. This theme is amplified nicely by Mills in his chapter entitled "work"; see C. Wright Mills, *White Collar* (New York: Oxford University Press, 1951), pp. 215-238.
3. *Ibid.*, p. 238.
4. Philip Roth, *The Breast* (New York: Holt, Rinehart and Winston, 1972).

tive, sexually hungry breast. Yes, a female breast! Wouldn't the epitome of happiness be attained if you were transformed into a giant female breast? Your massive nipple could be fondled and caressed twenty-four hours a day. Nothing to do but pulsate and enjoy.

But what kind of existence would that be? Despite the euphoria of constant sexual stimulation, would such an existence be all that different from that of a beetle? Yet, as some Americans have learned, including even a few of high school and college ages, through numerous mood-altering devices that are readily available, retreatism into a private stupor is possible, at least for prolonged periods of time.

Of course, some reject this retreatist alternative. We have encountered students who really believe that a major political revolution is just around the corner. "Young people today will not accept life in large organizations. We refuse to become walking zombies." While we acknowledge their fervor, we doubt the validity of their prediction. Large organizations are not going to disappear in American society during your lifetime.

O.K. Granted that, what other options do we have? We can't escape by selecting a nonbusiness route. As we described earlier, organizations permeate all institutional sectors of American society. Deciding to seek the part of a teacher, minister, lawyer, doctor, accountant, or social worker is not an escape. These professionals and others like them work within large organizations too. Of course, the official norms permit much greater degrees of freedom for persons acting in such positions. Available research clearly demonstrates sharp conflicts between the professional expectations many hold and the tenets of bureaucracy with

which they are forced to live.[5] So don't be misled into thinking that you can totally escape the restrictiveness of organizational life by pursuing a professional career.

The stark reality remains for most American adults. As captives of an employee society, what do they experience? The daily grind, repeated hour after hour, day after day, then finally a weekend. Let's recognize that to many there does not appear to be a problem. "That's the way life is. Be grateful you're alive now and not fifty years ago, when things were a hell of a lot tougher." Many who accept this view are older and still recall the Depression of the thirties, and before that their parent's struggles. And they are absolutely right! The ranges of freedom experienced by the mass of American citizens today are perhaps greater than ever before in the history of the nation. Compared to the past, no child born today, even if she is black or Chicano, confronts threats to life and liberty as severe as those of their parents or grandparents.

However, the deficiencies of the past do not legitimate the present, at least not for some. Who are the critics? Only the young? Interestingly enough, age does not appear to be the decisive variable. Rather, contact with colleges and universities, either personal or through one's children, is far more important.[6] Persons who have had such contact are much more critical of the ethic that

5. Ronald G. Corwin, *Militant Professionalism* (New York: Appleton-Century-Crofts, 1970); James E. Sorensen, "Professional and Organizational Profiles of the Migrating and Non-Migrating Large Public Accounting Firm CPA," *Decision Sciences* 1 (July-October, 1970): 489-512.

6. Daniel Yankelovich, "Counterculture vs. Conservatism," *The Denver Post*, February 18, 1973, p. 37; see also Daniel Yankelovich, Inc., *The Changing Values of Campus: Political and Personal Attitudes of Today's College Students* (New York: Washington Square Press, 1972).

appears predominant today. What is this ethic? Depending on the bias of the speaker it may be labeled variously "The Work Ethic" or "The Living Dead." Regardless of the label, however, the central theme is the same. That is, "Accept your job as a job—it's a sacrifice you make to earn the money you need to do the things you really want to do."

Of course, many who accept this ethic hear the criticisms voiced by those who reject it; misunderstand their argument; and often respond with rage. "Damned kids, none of them want to work! They've had a free ride all of these years and they're spoiled rotten; think they're too damned good to have to work. They'll probably all end up going on welfare." Ever heard it before? Then, of course, the second stanza may be shouted, "It's our schools. They teach them that an honest day's work isn't worth a damn. But what can you expect—most of them never worked a day in their life either."

You may have decided that our speaker is correct. Many have. If you agree, then American society, as it is organized presently, must look awfully good. If only something could be done about those misguided souls who don't want jobs. Who misleads them anyway? Are our schools really failing? If you subscribe to this view they may very well be. Of course, if you disagree with it, then the discontent with work in America that may in part be stimulated by colleges and universities may have a degree of legitimacy. But what is the basis of this discontent? What's wrong with working in a large organization anyway?

Three ideas may clarify the argument. First, production volumes made possible in part by large organizations do offer Americans an unprecedented material richness.

Despite the popularity of "simulated poverty," especially as reflected in much campus dress, we see nothing wrong with material items *per se*. The object of a "good life," as we see it, does not reside in imitating the poor. Furthermore, compared to the immediate past, the demands of most jobs today are far less inhumane. Working conditions, wages, fringe benefits, hours, and the like, reflect improvement.

Second, for many, the alienation implicit in accepting "a job as a job" is a preferred mode of living. For some this adaption will not become problematic at any time throughout their life. "This job pays well and I'm doing it for the money. Well, not really the money, but the things money can buy."

Of course, some who have accepted this view early in life have later experienced a crisis. At times it was precipitated through probing questions and hostile interactions with their college-aged children, who, like other adolescents before them, can demonstrate a remarkable ability at insulting, ridiculing, and demeaning the life style and values of their parents. Thus, some who have accepted this view of work do so because they have never really thought about it nor have they been confronted with alternatives. They fail to recognize that the fundamental problem with this "leisure solution"—". . . it underestimates the fact that work remains the single most important life activity for most people . . . ."[7] And so one morning they wake up; hear the birds outside their window; see the sunlight streaming in; and find that they have been transformed into a beetle.

For many, however, death comes prior to metamorphosis. They really never question

7. Robert Blauner, *Alienation and Freedom: The Factory Worker and His Industry* (Chicago: University of Chicago Press, 1964), pp. 183-184.

the daily grind. Oh, they may complain a lot, but that's a lot easier than serious questioning. Let's face it. This happens to most who really need the direction and structure offered by their organizational position. Self-structuring would be too frightening. Pondering fundamental questions about the meaning and purpose of their life is simply too upsetting. Without the organizational script which dictates arrival at 8:00 a.m., how would their day begin? If their job is viewed solely as a means to enable them to pursue leisure activities, we would not expect them to get to work until the bell rang. And they wouldn't, unless the job meant more. Of course, after the pattern is repeated for several years, it becomes self-sustaining—7:25 a.m. the car engine starts almost automatically.

Third, we suspect that the work ethic in America is being transformed. At the vanguard of this process are some who have attended college. Of course, for many this period was simply one long series of examinations over material in which they had little interest. Thinking about the implications of philosophy, biology, or economics, especially for their own life, simply did not occur. Thus, they may be trained for something, but they have yet to learn what education is all about.

Others, however, have become more aware. Aware of who they are, how they got that way, and who they want to try and become. It is among this group, "contaminated" by the humanistic insights of past thinkers, who find the assembly line most hateful. *The work ethic is being transformed, but that does not mean that persons no longer want to work.* Rather they want to work, really invest themselves into activities to which they can be committed. A job may be a necessary evil, something done for as

short a time as possible until one can find *real* work. Or rather, a job at which one *can* work. Not just to earn money to buy a television set or to go to a football game; not that there is anything wrong with doing either. But for a job to provide work, in this newer meaning of the term, it must permit an investment of self. Otherwise, participants sharing this definition, experience intense alienation as they attempt to "play" the part, but remain less attached to it than even a stage actor in a melodrama. See how the observation, or complaint if you wish, made about many college graduates by employers has validity? Seeing individuals "play acting" in organizational positions about which you attach more importance is hard to take. And it matters not whether you are a department manager at J. C. Penney Company, a university professor, or the recipient of an engagement ring. If you value the part, seeing someone "play acting" can only enrage.

In short, educated persons do want to work. Their definition of the meaning of work is not really new, however. It reflects many of the values subscribed to by the craftsmen of the past. Numerous surveys indicate that this changed view of work is not restricted to a few "ivory tower" intellectuals. For example, "The University of Michigan Survey Research Center asked 1,533 working people to rank various aspects of work in order of importance. 'Good pay' came in a distant fifth, behind 'interesting work,' 'enough help and equipment to get the job done,' 'enough information to do the job,' and 'enough authority to do the job.'"[8] But pride in, and commitment to

8. Donald M. Morrison, "Is the Work Ethic Going Out of Style?" *Time* 100 (October 30, 1972): 97.

one's work requires many things that are simply not possible within the structural patterns characterizing many American organizations today. So some set up their own craft shops reminiscent of earlier artisans. Of course, without the purchasing power of their customers who work in large organizations, they would fold quickly. Thus, this type of solution can be made available only for a few. And the rest? By and large they accept jobs elsewhere, only to find the restrictions overwhelming. Like what? Let's look at a few.

ORGANIZATIONS ARE RESTRICTIVE

Yes, they are! Recall being in elementary school and having to ask permission to get out of your seat? "In most auto assembly plants, a worker must even get permission from his foreman before he can go to the bathroom."[9] And other places we have heard of have time limits for such visits as well as rules that preclude taking reading material along. Why? Because they were needed to curb worker abuse. But persons enacting positions for which they have little respect or self-investment are amazingly creative at finding ways around such rules. Recall our examples of unofficial norms? What's a supervisor to do?

Most visible are time restrictions; there is a time to be at work, a time for coffee breaks, a time for lunch, and so on. Children in some elementary schools are conditioned early to accept such a day. We have noted schedules in many where activities are arranged by the minute and have listened to some teachers who assure us with intensity that they see to it that their class begins reading at 10:06 a.m. and spelling at 10:38 a.m. However, there is another side. Time restrictions are essen-

tial if the activities of hundreds are to be coordinated in the most efficient manner. Telephones must be answered, and teachers need to be present when first graders arrive. The tension is inherent, to a degree at least so long as we seek to produce less costly goods and services.

Spontaneity of interaction is largely curtailed within any organization. Primary school children learn, eventually, to raise their hands. Once assigned to any position within an organization, you too will learn quickly who you are permitted to talk with and when. You don't wander around the building in a carefree manner; your movements are restricted. You have no business appearing in most offices and such behavior will not be tolerated for very long.

Yet these restrictions are just a beginning. Recall our earlier discussion in Chapter 3 of the dimensions of roles and positions? As an organizational participant, you will become aware of norms, both official and unofficial, that specify the ranges of tolerable behaviors for persons enacting your position. Task behaviors and authority relationships are spelled out. Recall status norms? Not only will the norms guide you in specifying to whom you may speak, about what and when, but also the proper tone of voice and form of address will be specified. Maybe even the type of clothing that you must wear will be designated so that others will know your prestige level at first glance. For most organizational participants, the normative structures they confront are rather tight. Freedom of movement in the broadest sense of the term is highly restricted to insure adequate control and coordination. Some structures are incredibly so. But need they be? Why?

9. *Ibid.*, p. 8

QUESTIONING THE UNQUESTIONABLE

Recognizing the intensity and scope of the type of critique we briefly summarized above, some officials have begun to experiment with alternative types of normative structures. Although the specifics vary immensely depending upon the type of task, the general theme is clear: Redesign patterns of official norms to permit more freedom of action by participants. Gradually, some managers are recognizing the need for "self-renewal," both for individuals and organizational structures.[10] Former structural arrangements were designed to fit a population that was largely untrained and not prepared to assume much responsibility for self-direction or self-education. Remember our discussion of this in Chapter 2? At that time these managerial philosophies worked, but new skill levels and more humanistic expectations now demand major changes. As one personnel manager put it: "We have run out of dumb people to handle those dumb jobs. So we have to rethink what we are doing."[11]

Thus, in contrast to the logic of Taylor's "Principles of Scientific Management," many tasks are being combined instead of being further subdivided. Example: "In compiling its telephone books, Indiana Bell used to divide 17 separate operations among a staff of women. The company gradually changed, giving each worker her own directory and making her responsible for all 17 tasks, from scheduling to proofreading. Results: work force turnover dropped, and errors, absenteeism and overtime declined."[12] Even the sacred assembly line process for automobile construction is being reviewed. Perhaps you've noticed ads like these: "BORED PEOPLE BUILD BAD CARS. THAT'S WHY WE'RE DOING AWAY WITH THE ASSEMBLY LINE. Working on an assembly line is monotonous. And boring. And after a while, some people begin not to care about their jobs anymore. So the quality of the product often suffers."[13]

So much rhetoric? Of course! Recall how participants seek to use symbols like this to affect our image of their organization and their products? But the fact that this line of persuasion is used tells us a good deal about changed meanings of work. Such meanings are not uniform throughout all varieties of organizations, nor do they simply reflect use of technology. The issue is far more complex as a few analysts have begun to discover upon comparing different types of organizations wherein new technologies have greatly changed worker activities. For example, Blauner concluded: "Social alienation is widespread in the automobile industry because of the marked anomic tendencies inherent in its technology and work organization. In the chemical industry, on the other hand, continuous-process technology and more favorable economic conditions result in a social structure with a high degree of consensus between workers and management and an integrated industrial community in which employees experience a sense of belonging and membership."[14]

There are other means being tried to alter work environments. For example, to a limited extent some workers are encouraged to organize their own work. Also, since many items require actions by several different

10. John Gardner, *Self Renewal: The Individual and the Innovative Society* (New York: Harper Colophon Books, Harper & Row Publishers, 1965).

11. Morrison, "Is the Work Ethic Going Out of Style?," p. 97.

12. *Ibid.*

13. Appeared in *Time* 101 (March, 1973): 7.

14. Blauner, *Alienation and Freedom*, p. 178.

types of specialists, allowing each to review the final product may have a multitude of consequences. And time restrictions? Are there any options? "In West Germany, some 3,500 firms have adopted 'sliding time.' In one form of the plan, company doors are open from 7 a.m. until 7 p.m., and factory or office workers can come in any time they like, provided that they are around for 'core time,' from 10 a.m. to 3 p.m., and they put in a 40-hour week."[15] The same basic pattern of flexibility has been adopted by several large U.S. firms in recent years.

These are just a few concrete examples of how many organizational managers are responding to this problem. Based on empirical research data that has been synthesized by such theorists as Likert,[16] McGregor,[17] and Argyris,[18] workers are beginning to be treated more like adults. The split between work and leisure becomes reduced as life emerges as a whole. That doesn't mean that individuals must not go fishing or enjoy a football game on TV. But it does mean that one's job becomes one's work, an important and cherished aspect of one's life. With such changes, many jobs are moved a bit closer toward approximating the craftsmen pattern of an earlier era wherein their work, play, and leisure were complementary rather than competing. "Play is something you do to be happily occupied, but if work occupies you happily, it is also play, although is it also serious, just as play is to a child."[19]

At this point, some "human relations" theorists, as they are often labeled, get carried away. Their enthusiasm is so intense that you get the impression that by next week, or next month at the latest, America will be transformed into a society of happy, contented, self-renewing workers who will be involved busily in redesigning their work

environments. Unfortunately, such changes occur only in Hollywood movies, and even there they are increasingly rare.

While there are many reasons why such a simplistic prediction will prove wrong, let's look at three fundamental ones. First, despite many innovations at all levels of American education, students—be they enrolled in kindergarten or college—are too often taught in tightly organized bureaucracies rather than being encouraged to participate in designing their own educational experiences.[20] Although this too is changing, many persons remain like the Parisian office workers studied by Crozier—they simply do not know how to participate in such decision-making activities and seek to avoid them.[21]

Second, as we mentioned briefly in Chapter 4, the degree of uncertainty in the technology used, and several other factors, create differing levels of interdependency among participants. When the actions taken by one group greatly affect a series of other divisions throughout the organization, then tighter control mechanisms can be expected.

15. Morrison, "Is the Work Ethic Going Out of Style?," p. 97.

16. Rensis Likert, *The Human Organization* (New York: McGraw-Hill Book Company, 1967) and *New Patterns of Management* (New York: McGraw-Hill Book Company, 1961).

17. Douglas McGregor, *The Human Side of Enterprise* (New York: McGraw-Hill Book Company, 1960) and Caroline McGregor and Warren G. Bennis (eds.), *The Professional Manager* (New York: McGraw-Hill Book Company, 1967).

18. Chris Argyris, *Integrating the Individual and the Organization* (New York: John Wiley & Sons, Inc., 1964) and *The Applicability of Organizational Sociology* (Cambridge, Mass.: Cambridge University Press, 1972).

19. Mills, *White Collar*, p. 222.

20. Charles E. Silberman, *Crisis in the Classroom* (New York: Random House, 1970).

21. Michel Crozier, *The World of the Office Worker*, trans. David Landau (Chicago: University of Chicago Press, 1971), pp. 153-160.

Thus, there are severe limits to participation in decision making, especially for many types of tasks. The rhetoric of "human relations theory" better fits some types of organizations than others.

Third, social inequality is reflected in several different types of behaviors ranging from autonomy, e.g., freedom of movement for professional vs. assemblyline workers; to security, e.g., salary levels and stock options for corporate executives vs. garbagemen who have little or no reserves; to prestige, e.g., country club membership vs. the neighborhood bar. Some theorists have argued that such differentials provide an important motivational function, and that competition for these desired positions helps to insure that they will be filled only by the most capable.[22] Of course, this interpretation has had its critics, but we see little evidence that existing levels of social inequality are about to disappear.[23] Indeed, managerial training in human relations skills of varied assortments, including sensitivity training, encounter groups and the like, is being used as a powerful weapon to insure continuity. Thus, some have argued, like labor organizers of old, that power remains concentrated, and until that is changed, all the rest is illusion. And so they seek ways to alter the structure of authority so that power might be redistributed to some degree. Through such restructuring, the degrees of individual choice and discretion might be broadened. But there is no clear-cut model to follow; and those with power and privilege have little incentive to endorse redistribution. Thus, the future will be one of experimentation and conflict reflecting diverse interests and values.

What are the implications of all of this for you personally? Think about it; for it is a matter which only you can decide.

HAVING YOUR CAKE AND EATING IT TOO

No one can tell you what constitutes "the good life" for you. That is a matter that each of us must decide privately. The best that anyone else can do is to raise issues that may stimulate you to think about your existence, both past and future, in ways that you might not otherwise. There are many options and many coping patterns. But there are realities too. However, too often they remain illusive or totally unrecognized. Our central objective in writing this short book has been to help you to increase your capacity to perceive some of these, and thereby increase your freedom to act. Unrecognized, they serve as powerful constraints on your behavior. Once perceived, you can begin to make choices as to which of the many constraints you wish to accept and which you think ought to be changed. That is the critical point. Change is possible—rarely as rapid as we wish, but with hard work and persistence, it can occur. Not everywhere all at once, but faster in many spheres than most of us dare hope at times.

Four warnings before we proceed, however. First, don't expect to find a set of simple answers in the concluding comments that follow. They aren't there, nor elsewhere, actually. Second, don't be surprised when you set out to try to change some aspect of a group's functioning or an organizational procedure, and then discover that

22. Kingsley Davis and Wilbert E. Moore, "Some Principles of Stratification," *American Sociological Review* 10 (April, 1945): 242-249.

23. See for example, Melvin Tumin, "Some Principles of Stratification: A Critical Analysis," *American Sociological Review* 28 (August, 1953): 387-394; Walter Buckley, "On Equitable Inequality," *American Sociological Review* 28 (October, 1963): 790-800; and Wladzimierz Wesolowski, "Some Notes on the Functional Theory of Stratification," *The Polish Sociological Bulletin* 5-6 (1962): 64-69.

you meet intense resistance. Some may have much to lose if the *status quo* is altered. And the losses may be hard for you, or even them, to specify. Anticipate the resistance; undoubtedly it will be there. Third, don't be surprised to start out with an assumed injustice and then upon digging into it, learn that the situation is far more complex than you had thought. Networks of inter-organizational linkages create patterns of constraint that at one location may have negative consequences for individuals positioned there, but alteration may result in far more problems elsewhere. Like it or not, there comes a time to choose sides. Fourth, and finally, don't look for villains.[24] Charismatic individuals, defined as saints or devils, depending on your biases, are necessary. However, without changing structures, behavior patterns will maintain remarkable continuity despite replacement of top officials. Remember always Orwell's pigs who were even able to begin walking upright shortly after the farmers were removed.[25]

In all organizations there are strains and tensions. As an individual, learn to look for these and realize the private pains they can precipitate. Strain-free environments do not exist. That doesn't mean that we ought not to try and reduce them when we can, but recognize that you are going to have to learn to live with such contradictions and tensions. Understanding doesn't eradicate them, but it may make for a more bearable situation.

What is the domain of an organization? Remember that the expectation networks that comprise domains vary a great deal. You may prefer the freedoms permitted by a looser domain than a higher salary that might be offered by an official from an organization characterized by more restrictiveness. Of even greater importance is the central task of the organization. Is it one to which you can subscribe? If not, be careful.

Recall the simplistic criticisms and images of bureaucracies, red tape, and passing the buck. In the search for organizational structures that permit pluralism, i.e., differences of opinion to persist rather than be eradicated, official rules are constantly being established and made more formal. Recognize their necessity and the protections and freedoms they permit. However, these rules must always be questioned, and you must be prepared to engage in such questioning. We can expect to see an increase in this process as participants seek to expand the limits of tolerable behaviors and options available.

Recognize that what you are experiencing as a specific case, may very well reflect a broader public issue. For example, only a few years ago abortion was viewed by most as a form of deviance. Who are these criminals who seek abortions? What's wrong with their socialization? Where did their parents go wrong? And think of the guilt and shame you might have experienced if you discovered that your mother had one. See how the issue has been recast with a changed definition of the legal norm? Perhaps similar rule changes will redefine the meanings and evaluations attached to homosexual activity and possession of marijuana in the not too distant future. Thus, learn to look for links between private troubles experienced by individuals and broader public issues.[26]

24. Thomas E. Drabek and E. L. Quarantelli, "Scapegoats, Villains, and Disasters," *Trans-action*, 4 (March, 1967), pp. 12-17.

25. George Orwell, *Animal Farm* (New York: Signet, The New American Library, 1956).

26. C. Wright Mills, *The Sociological Imagination* (New York: Oxford University Press, 1959).

We can expect continuation of a similar process at the more general organizational level. To what degree can high school officials attempt to constrain student dress? For some, this will remain an important point of disagreement. The limits for students have been broadened greatly because a few cared enough to fight for a right they thought should be theirs. Similarly, the number of instances involving litigation over alleged sexual or ethnic discrimination will increase too, as a part of this general process which is societal wide. Recognize it as such, for new definitions for what constitutes discriminatory behavior are being created. Realize that it hurts when you have had good intentions, but discover that others have interpreted your behavior differently. The strains and anxieties that such wranglings reflect and produce are a fact of organizational life that all of us are going to have to learn to tolerate better. However, the expanded freedoms are worth the price, since uniform consensus is not possible and an autocratic or benevolent dictator not desirable.

Upon joining an organization, study it carefully. Ascertain the official normative structure and note areas of ambiguity and inconsistency. About which areas is there dissensus? What are the patterns among the resulting cleavages? Where do the normative and interpersonal structures clash? Which organizations in your immediate environment are seeking to extend their control over sectors of yours? Seek to ascertain quickly the unofficial norms that persons around you are using. Then proceed to *use* this knowledge to get done what you deem as top priority. In short, seek to understand your limits, test them with caution, and when necessary, push for redefinitions of the rules so that you can participate in a work environment that is more of your own creation. If committed to the organizational task you are trying to accomplish, such activities can result in the same sense of fulfillment and accomplishment that master craftsmen experience who work as individuals.

Big organizations are not undefeatable. We are going to see more Don Quixotes on the scene in the future. They will prick like pins, and on occasion organizational practices will be altered. Many law students and some lawyers undoubtedly will pursue the path forged by Ralph Nader and his "raiders." Such persons have helped all of us to learn that massive structures, highly formidable in appearance, may topple or bend if pushed. Thus, emerging into the arena of conflict and counterbalance that has long been dominated by business, labor, agricultural and governmental organizations, are civil rights groups, be they representing women, blacks, Chicanos, or homosexuals; environmental groups, e.g., Sierra Clubs; and general citizen's lobby groups, e.g., Common Cause. Recent examples of the accomplishments of such groups appear in the mass media daily. Many Americans are beginning to realize the power that a small collection of individuals with a narrow focus can muster. Perhaps you read of the decision not to hold the 1976 Olympic games in Colorado. Planning had begun and it seemed that there was little anyone could do even though many scattered throughout the state feared increased taxes and stimulation of population growth. But defeat came through an election referendum. Having gotten the issue on the ballot, the citizens voted to stop further state spending on the Olympics. Even the opponents of the Olympics were surprised by the margin of their victory. This illustration is simply an example of the type of activity through which future constraints will be placed on organizational officials by hostile groups who are opposed to their actions.

Once such activities were reserved for the elites. But increasingly greater proportions of Americans have the opportunities to participate on varied organizational stages. There are countless potentials and "impossible dreams." It is up to you to decide which ones mean enough to be given the most precious commodity you have to give —your time. Purpose and meaning can be forthcoming in any American community, but it must be initiated through actions taken by each individual. As we are instructed by Roth's hero who closes his narrative with some lines from a Rilke poem, "You must change your life."[27]

Looking out at these arenas of organized conflict, recognize that some of your peers will decide, perhaps only temporarily, to drop out. Recall Davis's analysis from Chapter 2? We suspect that such short-term departures will continue in the future, but that for most they will continue to be just that— short term. For some, these sojourns may be the type of educational experience, i.e., self-discovery, that others will gain through the intense intellectual challenging that sometimes is encountered on college campuses. Of course, the many types of risks that accompany life in a "counterculture" are grave, and the pains experienced by most parents of "lost children" are intense. However, we fully expect the pattern to continue, so don't be alarmed, or terrified, or conned into joining on the assumption that you will stay forever.

What stage are you on now? What part were you playing yesterday at this time? Remember the imagery we have introduced you to and try to use it. Seek to notate the behavior patterns that form the organizational systems in which you find yourself. Try to become better able to explicate the normative, interpersonal, and resource structures that enable persons to act on these stages in such patterned ways day after day. Note the strains within and among these structures and how persons seek to cope with them and endure the private pains that they inflict. Learn to step back and see what is happening around you. Having been helped to gain these insights through which your own personal freedom may be increased, then ask: "What can I do to alter the structures in which others find themselves so as to permit their lives to be freer?" And having made a decision, seek the courage to act.

For Further Reading

Argyris, Chris. *The Applicability of Organizational Sociology.* Cambridge, Mass.: Cambridge University Press, 1972.

Argyris critiques several theoretical positions recently advocated by sociologists, e.g., Blau, Perrow, and Thompson, and puts forth his own case for wider experimentation and application of a managerial philosophy based on treating workers as adults.

Bell, Daniel. *Work and Its Discontents.* Boston: Beacon Press, 1956.

A biting critique of the ethic of efficiency, Taylorism, and the altered work environments that such ideologies have produced.

Bennis, Warren. *American Bureaucracy.* New York: Aldine Publishing Company, 1970.

A diverse collection of analyses that have appeared over the past few years in the journal *Society Transaction* (formerly *Transaction,* which is read widely by specialists and nonspecialists alike.

Blauner, Robert. *Alienation and Freedom.* Chicago: University of Chicago Press, 1964.

An empirical study of printers, textile workers, automobile assembly line employees

27. Roth, *The Breast,* p. 87.

and chemical operators; their work environments, modes of technology, and differentiating levels of alienation are interrelated.

Davis, Fred. *On Youth Subcultures: The Hippie Variant*. New York: General Learning Press, 1971.

One of the few systematic analyses of the subjective definitions and external societal constraints that have given rise to youth subcultures.

Gardner, John. *Self-Renewal: The Individual and The Innovative Society*. New York: Harper Colophon Books, Harper & Row, 1965.

This inspirational and insightful essay, rich with instructions on the self-renewal process, will long remain a classic.

Jacobs, Paul. *Prelude to Riot: A View of Urban America From the Bottom*. New York: Vintage Books, 1966.

The deficiencies of big city bureaucracies, including police, welfare, employment, housing, educational, and health organizations are described with fervor, at times outrage.

Mills, C. Wright. *White Collar: The American Middle Classes*. New York: Oxford University Press, 1951.

Historical interpretation and biting critique of American society, middle class occupations, and emergent life styles.

Research and Policy Committee of the Committee for Economic Development. *Social Responsibilities of Business Corporations*. New York: Committee for Economic Development, 1971.

An assessment of the emergent public responsibilities of large corporations in a changed American society wherein there is increased sensitivity to the reciprocal impacts of organizational-community interactions.

Glossary

Alienation—A feeling of not being fully involved in a particular social unit such as a group (e.g., family), organization (e.g., university), or community. Feelings of despair, helplessness, powerlessness, and a sense of social isolation are aspects of this variable.

Authority—Specifies power relationships which have been accepted as legitimate or morally right. Weber differentiated three types of authority which reflected different bases: traditional, charismatic, and rational-legal (see definitions for each).

Autonomy—The degree to which a social unit is internally directed and free from external constraints or regulation.

Boundary—The borderline between two social systems given a particular criterion, e.g., frequency of interaction, limits of authority, or content of interaction.

Bureaucracy—A special type or form of social organization characterized by such criteria as a high division of labor that is hierarchially structured, formal rules which define authority relationships and tasks, impersonality among participants, and assignment to positions on the basis of technical competence.

Bureaucratization—The process by which a social unit is transformed into a bureaucracy, i.e., becomes restructured so as to reflect a specified set of analytic criteria, e.g., formalization, division of labor, and the like.

Centralization—A structural feature of any social unit which refers to the degree to which members participate in such activities as decision making and communication, e.g., in highly centralized organizations most decisions are made by persons at, or near the top.

Charismatic Authority—A social relationship in which power has been accepted as legitimate or morally right because of the qualities of an individual, e.g., a brilliant leader of a religious sect, or political movement.

Complexity—A structural feature of an organization that refers to the degree of differentiation of tasks in both a horizontal and vertical sense.

Complex Organization—A relatively permanent and relatively complex discernible interaction system.

Consensus—Agreement among persons; especially in organizations, about expectations regarding the tasks, authority relationships, modes of deference and sanctioning, that should occur among persons enacting social positions.

Co-optation—The process of formally appointing or otherwise including within an organization outsiders that might pose a threat, e.g., police department officials might appoint a leader from a militant ethic group to a task force on police-community relations.

Domain—Normative expectations pertaining to an entire system or subsystem of actors, e.g., mission norms specify central tasks, thus, one should go to a bank for a loan not a fire department.

Environment—Anything that is not included within the organizational boundary, e.g., other local organizations, socioeconomic characteristics of the community in which the organization is located, and regulatory agencies at state or federal levels.

Formalization—A structural feature of organizations referring to the degree to which rules, usually written, are used to specify how, when, where, and for what purposes, participants are to interact.

Formal Organization—A social unit characterized by a high degree of formalization.

Human Relations Theory—A managerial ideology which emphasizes that organizational productivity will be increased if the importance of social relations among participants is recognized and if members are encouraged to participate in decisions regarding the ordering of their work activity.

Interaction System—Any unit of human interaction that is relatively enduring ranging from such simple and uncomplicated systems like brief encounters among strangers (gatherings) to more permanent units like families, gangs and work groups, to more complex systems like organizations, communities, and societies.

Interpersonal Structure—The entire collection of expectations, orientations, and understandings among participants which are person specific, i.e., not role or position based.

Norm—Expectations that define a range of tolerable behavior for a given social category of persons, e.g., students ought to turn in their work in accordance with the time deadlines set by their professors.

Normative Structure—The entire set or collection of norms that may be operative within an organization.

Official Norm—A norm which is authorized and enforced by various actors in positions of authority.

Organizational Strain — Inconsistencies among various organizational components; e.g., organizational norms might require that two individuals who dislike each other as persons must interact frequently; sometimes professors may be told to focus their energies on teaching and meeting with students, but then may be evaluated for tenure largely on the basis of published research.

Power—The ability of one individual or collection of individuals to have another individual or collection do something that the first wants done.

Rational-Legal Authority—A social relationship in which power has been accepted as legitimate or morally right because of a larger set of rules that designate a hierarchy of positions, e.g., any persons designated as foremen have the authority to direct certain activities of a prescribed collection of workers.

Resource Structure—All physical resources used by participants, their ecological placement, and relevant skills of participants.

Role—A cluster of norms which pertains to a given unit of social interaction, e.g., husband-wife, cook-waiter.

Routinization—A structural feature of organizations referring to the degree to which the central task process is predictable, stable, and certain, e.g., automobile manufacturing organization compared to a hospital for the mentally ill.

Sanction—A type of norm which specifies appropriate behaviors when there is rule violation, e.g., a hard stare, docking one's pay, firing an employee. Some writers stress what are labeled frequently as "positive sanctions," i.e., appropriate behaviors when there is consistent compliance with the rules, e.g., a raise, promotion, or other type of "pat on the back."

Social Position—The total collection of roles that are commonly thought to go together, e.g., husband, doctor, or waiter.

Status—A type of category of norms pertaining to social rank and ways in which it is expressed, e.g., nurses ought to address physicians as "doctor," business executives ought to have carpeted offices and attractive desks.

Traditional Authority—A social relationship in which power has been accepted as legitimate or morally right because of tradition, e.g., parental power over children reflects this.

Taylorism—A managerial ideology, often labeled "scientific management" after its founder, Frederick W. Taylor, which stresses the responsibility of managers to research alternative work patterns through such techniques as "time and motion" study, to plan and subdivide work activity into highly specialized tasks, to train workers in the best way to perform such, and to pay workers on "piece rate" or quota systems so that those with the greatest output will receive maximum wages.

Unofficial Norm—A norm which is not officially recognized or enforced by persons occupying positions at a given level in an organization.

Index

Abrahamson, Mark, 68
activism, as orientation toward environment, 87
Aldrich, Howard E., 82
alienation, 34, 50, 97-99
   and technology, 101
   from jobs, 98-99
   from organizations, 97-99
allies, in organizational networks, 82
America. See United States of America
American Farm Bureau Federation, 26
American Federation of Labor, 21
American Medical Association, 23
American Sugar Refining Company, 21
American Tobacco Company, 21
Anderson, Charles H., 33
Arendt, Hannah, 16
Argyris, Chris, 102, 106
Atomic Energy Commission, 28
authority, 10-16, 43, 75-79, 86
   as dimension of role, 43
   charismatic, 13
   in environmental relationships, 86
   rational-legal, 13-16
   relationships, among organizations, 75-79
   traditional, 12
authoritarian organizations, 54-56
   characteristics of, 55-56
autonomy, as organizational value, 85, 87-88, 91, 94

"back stage," as restricted areas within
   organizations, 6, 40
Baldridge, J. Victor, 94
bargaining, 50
Barker, Robert G., 53
Barnes, Henry A., 1
Beatrice Foods Company, 75-77
behavior pattern, analysis of, 1-4, 7-8, 38-41, 50-52
Bell, Daniel, 106
Bell, Gerald D., 68
Bendix, Reinhard, 11, 13, 17, 36
Bennett, Ruth, 59

Bennis, Warren G., 102, 106
Berkeley student revolt, 34
Berle, Adolf A., Jr., 25
Blau, Peter M., 8, 14, 53, 66
Blauner, Robert, 98, 101, 106
Boulding, Kenneth E., 36
boundaries, organizational, 5-7, 16-17, 40, 59-60,
   62, 74
boundary, in total organizations, 59-60
   in voluntary organizations, 62
   norms, 6-7
Bowers, Raymond V., 68
Breed, Warren, 53
Brown vs. Board of Education of Topeka, Kansas,
   29
Buckley, Walter, 103
budgeting process, as type of control in
   interorganizational network, 77-79
bureaucracy, 13-17, 22
   as ideal type, 13-17
   characteristics of, 17
   emergence in U. S. cities, 22
   emergence in U. S. state governments, 22
   emergence in U. S. schools, 22
   original meaning, 13-14
   stereotype, 14
Burkey, Richard M., 19, 31

Calvinism, 18, 24
Camus, Albert, 34
capitalistic ethos, 18-19
careers, within organizations, 16-17
change, strategies of effecting, 103-106
charismatic authority, 13
civil rights movement, 30
Clark, Burton R., 86
clients, in organizational networks, 80
Commission on Educational Reconstruction, 92
community disaster, organizational response, 93-94
competing organizations, 62-64
   characteristics of, 63-64

vertical, 74-79
interorganizational relations, in community
	disaster, 94
interpersonal structure, defined, 45

Jacobs, Paul, 107
Janowitz, Morris, 56
jobs, orientation toward, 96-99
	vs. leisure, 96-99
	vs. work, 99
Johnson, Lyndon B., 30-32
Johnson, Norman J., 66, 68
Jones, R. W., Jr., 63
Junker, B. H., 63

Kafka, Franz, 96
Kahn, Robert L., 9, 51
Kates, Robert W., 93
Katz, Daniel, 9
Katz, Michael, 22
Kennedy, John F., 30
Keniston, Kenneth, 34
King, Martin Luther, Jr., 29-30
Knights of Labor, 20-21
Knott, Paul, 34

labor unions, 20-21, 26-27, 92
	among government employees, 92
	as organizational threat, 92
	emergence of, 20-21
LaFollette, Robert M., 22
Laidler, H. W., 25
Leavitt, Harold J., 9
legitimation, 12-13
leisure, orientation toward, 96-99
	vs. jobs, 96-99
Lenski, Gerhard, 10, 36
Lenski, Jean, 10, 36
Lewis, John L., 26
Likert, Rensis, 102
Little, Roger W., 56

McGregor, Caroline, 102
McGregor, Douglas, 102
March, James G., 9
materialism, as American value, 33-36
Means, Gardiner C., 21, 25
mergers, 21, 25, 33, 64
metropolitanization, 32
Meyer, Marshall W., 8
Michels, Robert, 61
military-industrial complex, 29
Mills, C. Wright, 11, 96, 102, 104, 107
monopolistic organizations, 64-65
	characteristics of, 64-65
Moore, Wilbert E., 11, 83, 103
Morrison, Donald M., 99-101
muckrackers, 21-22

Nadel, S. F., 12
Nahemow, Lucille, 59
Nathan, Robert, 17
National Farmers Union, 26
National Labor Relations Board, 26
Nieburg, H. L., 33
Nixon, Richard M., 30-32
nonviolent resistance, 30
normative consensus and friction, 51
normative structure, 41-44, 49
	variations in, 49
norms, 5, 6-7, 41-49, 51-52
	boundary, 6-7
	defined, 41
	official, 47
	unofficial, 47-49, 52, 100

official norms, 52
	as restrictions, 100
	defined, 47
Office of Management and Budget (OMB), 77-79
opportunism, as orientation toward environment,
	86-87
organization set, 79-82
	allies, 82
	clients, 80
	competitors, 80-81
	customers, 80
	regulators, 81
	suppliers, 80
organizational boundary, 5-7, 16-17, 40, 59-60,
	62, 74
organizational change, strategies of effecting,
	103-106
organizational environment, see environment,
	organizational
organizational interdependence, 70, 72
organizational strain, 45, 48, 50-52, 104-105
	consequences of, 50-52
	defined, 50
organizational task, 8, 40, 43
organizations, as stages, 4-5, 7-8
	defined, 2, 41
	variations in, 2-3, 54-68
Orwell, George, 34, 104

Parsons, Talcott, 11, 66
Pasamanick, Benjamin, 59
Perrow, Charles, 64, 66-67, 95
policy setting, as type of control in
	interorganizational network, 77-79
position, social, 41-44, 52
	defined, 41
power, 11-13, 85-86, 91
	as environmental control, 91
power means, strategies of environmental control,
	85-86
Preiss, Jack J., 51

  total organizations, 58-60
    voluntary organizations, 60-62
voluntary organizations, 60-62
  characteristics of, 60-62

Warren, Ronald L., 83
weans, 17
Webb, Charles, 35
Weber, Max, 10-19, 24, 36
Weick, Karl E., 9
Wesolowski, Wladzimierz, 103
Whyte, William H., Jr., 34
Whyte, William F., 53

Williams, Robin M., Jr., 36
Wilson, Woodrow, 23
Wittich, Claus, 11
Wood, James R., 79, 87
Woodward, Joan, 67
work ethic, 98-99
work, orientation toward, 96-99
  vs. jobs, 99

Yankelovich, Daniel, 97

Zald, Mayer, 95
Zeitlin, Maurice, 21, 37